OPPOSING
VIEWPOINTS®
SERIES

Multiracial America

Other Books of Related Interest:

At Issue Series

The Children of Undocumented Immigrants

Global Viewpoints Series

Adoption

Social Networking

Opposing Viewpoints Series

The Millennial Generation

Racial Profiling

"Congress shall make
no law . . . abridging
the freedom of speech,
or of the press."

First Amendment to the US Constitution

The basic foundation of our democracy is the First Amendment guarantee of freedom of expression. The Opposing Viewpoints series is dedicated to the concept of this basic freedom and the idea that it is more important to practice it than to enshrine it.

Multiracial America

Noah Berlatsky and Lynn M. Zott

GREENHAVEN PRESS
A part of Gale, Cengage Learning

Detroit • New York • San Francisco • New Haven, Conn • Waterville, Maine • London

Elizabeth Des Chenes, *Director, Content Strategy*
Cynthia Sanner, *Publisher*
Douglas Dentino, *Manager, New Product*

For more information, contact:
Greenhaven Press
27500 Drake Rd.
Farmington Hills, MI 48331-3535
Or you can visit our Internet site at gale.cengage.com

For product information and technology assistance, contact us at

Gale Customer Support, 1-800-877-4253
For permission to use material from this text or product, submit all requests online at www.cengage.com/permissions

Further permissions questions can be emailed to permissionrequest@cengage.com

Articles in Greenhaven Press anthologies are often edited for length to meet page requirements. In addition, original titles of these works are changed to clearly present the main thesis and to explicitly indicate the author's opinion. Every effort is made to ensure that Greenhaven Press accurately reflects the original intent of the authors. Every effort has been made to trace the owners of copyrighted material.

© RTimages/Shutterstock.com

LIBRARY OF CONGRESS CATALOGING-IN-PUBLICATION DATA

Multiracial America / Noah Berlatsky and Lynn M. Zott, book editors.
    p. cm. -- (Opposing viewpoints)
    Includes bibliographical references and index.
    ISBN 978-0-7377-6662-2 (hardcover) -- ISBN 978-0-7377-6663-9 (pbk.)
    1. United States--Race relations--Political aspects. 2. Racially mixed people--United States. I. Berlatsky, Noah. II. Zott, Lynn M. (Lynn Marie), 1969-
    E184.A1M88 2014
    305.800973--dc23
                                                                    2013009080

Printed in the United States of America
1 2 3 4 5 6 7 17 16 15 14 13

Contents

Chapter 3: What Issues Surround Multiracial Relationships in America?

Chapter 4: What Issues Confront Children in Multiracial Families?

Why Consider Opposing Viewpoints?

> *"The only way in which a human being can make some approach to knowing the whole of a subject is by hearing what can be said about it by persons of every variety of opinion and studying all modes in which it can be looked at by every character of mind. No wise man ever acquired his wisdom in any mode but this."*
>
> *John Stuart Mill*

In our media-intensive culture it is not difficult to find differing opinions. Thousands of newspapers and magazines and dozens of radio and television talk shows resound with differing points of view. The difficulty lies in deciding which opinion to agree with and which "experts" seem the most credible. The more inundated we become with differing opinions and claims, the more essential it is to hone critical reading and thinking skills to evaluate these ideas. Opposing Viewpoints books address this problem directly by presenting stimulating debates that can be used to enhance and teach these skills. The varied opinions contained in each book examine many different aspects of a single issue. While examining these conveniently edited opposing views, readers can develop critical thinking skills such as the ability to compare and contrast authors' credibility, facts, argumentation styles, use of persuasive techniques, and other stylistic tools. In short, the Opposing Viewpoints Series is an ideal way to attain the higher-level thinking and reading skills so essential in a culture of diverse and contradictory opinions.

In addition to providing a tool for critical thinking, Opposing Viewpoints books challenge readers to question their own strongly held opinions and assumptions. Most people form their opinions on the basis of upbringing, peer pressure, and personal, cultural, or professional bias. By reading carefully balanced opposing views, readers must directly confront new ideas as well as the opinions of those with whom they disagree. This is not to argue simplistically that everyone who reads opposing views will—or should—change his or her opinion. Instead, the series enhances readers' understanding of their own views by encouraging confrontation with opposing ideas. Careful examination of others' views can lead to the readers' understanding of the logical inconsistencies in their own opinions, perspective on why they hold an opinion, and the consideration of the possibility that their opinion requires further evaluation.

Evaluating Other Opinions

To ensure that this type of examination occurs, Opposing Viewpoints books present all types of opinions. Prominent spokespeople on different sides of each issue as well as well-known professionals from many disciplines challenge the reader. An additional goal of the series is to provide a forum for other, less known, or even unpopular viewpoints. The opinion of an ordinary person who has had to make the decision to cut off life support from a terminally ill relative, for example, may be just as valuable and provide just as much insight as a medical ethicist's professional opinion. The editors have two additional purposes in including these less known views. One, the editors encourage readers to respect others' opinions—even when not enhanced by professional credibility. It is only by reading or listening to and objectively evaluating others' ideas that one can determine whether they are worthy of consideration. Two, the inclusion of such viewpoints encourages the important critical thinking skill of objectively evaluating an author's credentials and bias. This evaluation will illuminate an author's reasons for taking a particular stance on an issue and will aid in readers' evaluation of the author's ideas.

It is our hope that these books will give readers a deeper understanding of the issues debated and an appreciation of the complexity of even seemingly simple issues when good and honest people disagree. This awareness is particularly important in a democratic society such as ours in which people enter into public debate to determine the common good. Those with whom one disagrees should not be regarded as enemies but rather as people whose views deserve careful examination and may shed light on one's own.

Thomas Jefferson once said that "difference of opinion leads to inquiry, and inquiry to truth." Jefferson, a broadly educated man, argued that "if a nation expects to be ignorant and free . . . it expects what never was and never will be." As individuals and as a nation, it is imperative that we consider the opinions of others and examine them with skill and discernment. The Opposing Viewpoints series is intended to help readers achieve this goal.

David L. Bender and Bruno Leone,
Founders

Introduction

"White guy and Asian American woman. The combination may be the most common depiction of mixed-race couples in popular culture; African Americans are rarely glimpsed with white mates in TV shows or commercials, for example. It may even be more common than an Asian American man paired with an Asian American woman."

—Paul Farhi,
"Familiar Ad Trope: Pairing White Men and Asian American Women,"
Washington Post, *September 27, 2012*

Interracial, or mixed-race, relationships are increasingly common in the United States, but in some cases they remain controversial. The phenomenon of white men dating Asian women, for example, has generated much discussion and conflict within the Asian and Asian American communities.

Lauren sMash writes about her experiences as an Asian woman dating white men in a January 26, 2012, article at the *Persephone Magazine* blog. She says that some white men have "Yellow Fever"; by this she means that they "are obsessed with Asian women to the point that they rarely, if ever, date or enter into a sexual relationship with any other women." sMash says that at first when she was in college, she was flattered to realize that men found her attractive. But later, she began to realize that the white men who were attracted to her Asianness did not care about her as a person. She concludes:

> People with Yellow Fever don't want to get to know Asian women. In fact, I would venture to say that they don't care very much about Asian women at all. They are more con-

cerned with the idea of us—the notion that we are adorable little kawaii girls or demure lotus flowers or geisha-like sexual objects. Their attraction to Asian women relies on stereotypes that turn us into exotic sexual objects instead of real women. Stereotypes turn people like me into things that are measured against a caricature, and they strip me of the individuality that, frankly, I would probably have been more freely assigned if I were white. It is dehumanizing at best to constantly be compared to a stereotype and to have people chasing you not as a person, but as an embodiment of the stereotypes that they use to define you.

If white men sometimes fetishize Asian women, some Asian women idealize white men. As Vivienne Chen in a July 10, 2012, article in the *Huffington Post* argues, many Asian women like herself prefer white men because "we have grown up in a Western culture, with Western standards of beauty and Western ideals of romance. . . . *We prefer Western men because we grew up in a culture that prefers Western men.*"

Writer Jenny An goes further in an August 31, 2012, article at xoJane.com. An, who is an Asian woman, describes herself as a "racist" who dates only white men and not Asians. She says many Asian women deliberately want to reject their cultures, which emphasize deference to authority and career success. She also says that dating white men is a way to integrate, "to be true Americans." She adds:

> I date white men because the term "model minority" grosses me out. I date white men because it feels like I'm not ostracizing myself into an Asian ghetto and antiquated ideas of Asian unity. I still see myself as a minority. And with that, pretty soon comes connotations of "outsider." And I don't like that.

An notes that intermarriage between white men and Asian women has become very common, noting that 37 percent of recent Asian brides married a non-Asian. Despite such figures, however, Asian American women are actually starting to marry

Asian men at higher rates, according to a March 30, 2012, article by Rachel L. Swarns in the *New York Times*. Between 2008 and 2010, "the percentage of Asian-American newlyweds born in the US and who married someone of a different race dipped by nearly 10 percent," Swarns reports. Part of the change may be caused by increased immigration from Asian countries; there are simply more eligible Asian men from which to choose. But Asian couples that Swarns interviewed also said that sharing similar backgrounds had strengthened their relationships. For example, one woman appreciated that her husband was not put out when she suggested that, as is customary in some Asian cultures, her parents might live with them one day.

As the discussion around white male/Asian female couples shows, multiracial issues can generate strong and varied opinions. *Opposing Viewpoints: Multiracial America* explores some of these issues in chapters titled What Is the Connection Between Politics and Multiracial America?, How Can Multiracial America Become More Equal?, What Issues Surround Multiracial Relationships in America?, and What Issues Confront Children in Multiracial Families? As the United States becomes more diverse, these issues will be central for more and more people and for multiracial America as a whole.

CHAPTER 1

What Is the Connection Between Politics and Multiracial America?

Chapter Preface

Latinos are a growing percentage of the American electorate. In the 1992 US presidential election, Latinos made up only 4 percent of the electorate, according to a November 26, 2012, article in the *Huffington Post* by Manny Diaz and John Zogby. By 2004 Latinos had doubled their share of the vote to 8 percent. And in 2012, they made up around 10 percent of the electorate.

The growing influence of Latino voters has hurt the Republican Party significantly, especially as its share of that Latino vote has fallen. In 2004 Republican candidate George W. Bush won 40 percent of Latino votes on the way to election victory. In 2012 losing Republican candidate Mitt Romney scraped together only 29 percent of Latino votes.

In the wake of their 2012 loss, many leading Republicans argue that the party needs to improve its outreach to Latino voters. Specifically, they suggest that Mitt Romney's hard-line stance on immigration and his resistance to providing a path to citizenship for undocumented immigrants hurt his standing with Latino voters. Florida senator Marco Rubio asserts, "It's really hard to get people to listen to you . . . if they think you want to deport their grandmother," as quoted by Bill Hoffmann in a November 15, 2012, article for *Newsmax*. Rubio says he plans to back legislation to help undocumented immigrants who came to the United States as children. Other Republican leaders, such as Speaker of the House John Boehner and Sean Hannity, a conservative talk show host, also reversed earlier opposition to immigration reform and expressed support for a path to citizenship for illegal immigrants, according to Julia Preston in a November 9, 2012, article in the *New York Times*.

Other commentators, however, were skeptical that the change in immigration policy would significantly help Republicans with Latino voters. Matthew Yglesias, writing in a November 7, 2012, post for *Slate*, suggests that Latinos are driven away from the Republican Party not by any one specific policy but rather by a general attitude of racism and contempt toward nonwhite voters. Yglesias pointed especially to Republican opposition to the Supreme Court nomination of ethnic Puerto Rican Sonia Sotomayor. According to Yglesias, Republicans indulged in "mass racial panic" upon Sotomayor's nomination, accusing her of being a "'lightweight' who'd been coasting her whole life on the enormous privilege of growing up poor in the South Bronx." Kevin Drum, in a November 8, 2012, article for *Mother Jones* added:

> Lightening up on immigration won't be enough. Like it or not, conservatives are going to need a much more thorough housecleaning if they want to survive in an increasingly diverse future. No more gratuitous ethnic mockery. No more pretense that reverse racism is the *real* racism. No more suggestions that minorities just want a handout. . . . And no more too-clever-by-half attempts to say all this stuff without really saying it, and then pretending to be shocked when you're called on it. Pretending might make you feel virtuous, but it doesn't fool anyone and it won't win you any new supporters.

While commentators disagree on how Republicans should reach out to Hispanic voters, however, there is a general consensus that the Latino vote will only grow more important as it becomes a larger and larger percentage of the electorate. The viewpoints in this chapter will look at other ways in which the increasingly multiracial makeup of America and its citizens will affect US politics.

> "And because we now have a president
> with a different story than presidents
> past . . . each language and culture that
> is different is now more highly revered,
> as is each person's individual journey."

Barack Obama's Presidency Has Made Multiracial Americans More Accepted

Francesca Biller

Francesca Biller is a journalist and columnist who writes for the Huffington Post. In the following viewpoint, she discusses her experiences as a Japanese Jewish woman and argues that the 2008 election of President Barack Obama, a mixed-race individual, has been an inspiration for all mixed-race Americans. She says that Obama's election has helped her to overcome doubts about her own heritage and to see the worth of her own identity and of America's diversity.

As you read, consider the following questions:

1. What names does Biller say she was given, and how do they reflect her diverse heritage?

2. What quote does Biller single out from Obama's keynote address to the Democratic National Convention?

3. According to Biller, how did her parents meet?

As a Japanese-Jew, I have historically used self-deprecating humor at my own expense as a way to explain and defend to others who I was and to feel accepted.

Dignity and Class

My cultural confusion can be summed up in this anonymous quote, "There is no escaping karma. In a previous life, you never called, you never wrote, you never visited. And whose fault was that?"

Until recently I believed everything was my fault.

And I would certainly be the last person I would ever want to visit, with all of my kvetching to anyone kind enough to listen. "Oy Veh," I would lament. "No one accepts me; I am neither a truly Japanese or Jewish soul. I'll just sit here alone in the dark, eating a knish [a Jewish snack food] in my kimono [a Japanese robe]."

But gratefully, since [Barack] Obama has become president, not only do I feel more comfortable as the multiracial shikseh [non-Jewish woman] that I am, but engage in thoughtful conversations about my heritage and background, without jokes, defense or much self-deprecation.

I only hope that I conduct myself with an ounce of the class, genus and moral fortitude the president has displayed when continually questioned about his cultural identity.

In his keynote 2004 speech to the Democratic [National] Convention, Obama said, "In a sense I have no choice but to believe in this vision of America. As a child of a black man and a white woman, someone who was born in the racial melting pot of Hawaii, I've never had the option of restricting my loyalties on the basis of race, or measuring my worth on the basis of race."

I too was born in Hawaii and attended University High School in Hawaii a few years before Obama just a couple miles from his school, Punahoe High, whose students I shared long bus rides with from remote areas in order to get a good education; a value that my parents, like his, believed was invaluable.

Like my mother and father, Obama's parents are from two different cultures, yet he never feels the need to defend or justify his background; rather, he consistently responds to questions and assumptions with dignity and forethought.

When asked during the presidential campaign what he considered his ethnicity to be, Obama answered simply that he is an American from two equally rich and diverse cultures.

In a 2004 speech, Obama said, "My parents shared not only an improbable love; they shared an abiding faith in the possibilities of this nation. They would give me an African name, Barack, or blessed, believing that in a tolerant America your name is no barrier to success. They imagined me going to the best schools in the land, even though they weren't rich, because in a generous America you don't have to be rich to achieve your potential."

As a blend of cultures with a Jewish-Russian, Irish father and Japanese-Hawaiian mother, I too have faced continual questions as to what I considered my race, people, culture and ethnicity to be.

I was given several names, including three middle names, all five on my birth certificate. One is named after my Jewish great grandmother, Beatrice, the other a Japanese name, Yukari, and the third, Caitlin, named after the wife of my father's favorite poet, Dylan Thomas. My first name is named after a man—the Italian Renaissance painter, Piero Della Francesca, with his last name chosen for my first.

Who Was I?

Who was I, where did I come from, was I merely a mistake, an experiment, and how I might actually exist as an identifiable human—have been relentless questions that have sewn experiences throughout my culturally odd and unasked for politically patch-worked life.

This sentiment from an anonymous quote defines the neurotic dichotomy of my life, "To find the Buddha, look within. Deep inside you are ten thousand flowers. Each flower blossoms ten thousand times. Each blossom has ten thousand petals. You might want to see a specialist."

One searing memory I experienced involves a boy who told me on the school yard there was no such thing as a Japanese Jewish person. Afterwards, I ran all the way home from this boy with the piercing blue eyes and looked into the mirror wondering if I really didn't exist at all; at least in any real identifiable sense that mattered.

This was just one comment amongst countless surreal exclamations that secured my stalwart allegiance to defining myself as a person from different cultures, but never defined by them.

In his keynote speech to the Democratic National Convention, Obama said, "There is not a liberal America and a conservative America—there is the United States of America. There is not a Black America and a White America and Latino America and Asian America—there is the United States of America."

I can assume that President Obama has heard countless comments denying his existence as a fortified American as well, but was intrepid enough to remain an honorable candidate despite cultural ignorance on the part of others.

This is the essential definition for any strong person; the ability, will and might to face oppression and hatred and march forward anyway. Martin Luther King Jr. once said,

"Nothing in all the world is more dangerous than sincere ignorance and conscientious stupidity."

No one thought it was truly possible for a man who was Black to any degree to become president yet, no one. Some hoped, some feared, some dreamed, and many imagined a courageous, ambitious reality, but not one of us truly believed with full breadth that this young country was ready to make such a fearless leap for the betterment of us and for the world.

Chuppahs and Kimonos

Like Obama's parents, the marriage of my parents confounded some, upset others and was dismissed by the rest.

My father was raised in Los Angeles and then attended the University of Hawaii not long after the bombing of Pearl Harbor. He came back with an education and a wife, who was a second-generation Japanese-American known as the Nisei generation, who grew up as a farmer on the coffee plantations of Kona, Hawaii.

My Japanese-American uncles were part of the 442nd Infantry, also known as the Purple Heart Battalion, the most highly decorated fighter pilots in United States history. This includes some 4,000 bronze stars and nearly 9,500 Purple Hearts.

In this period, many Japanese-Americans were interned throughout the U.S, with land taken away, families torn apart and lives devastated, not unlike Jewish family members of my husband's during the Second World War with more tragic results.

A lot of anti-Japanese sentiment existed at this time, and yet my parents married, with whispers heard loudly as shouts and bombs from some family, while others chose to keep quiet with disdain; perhaps even more devastating.

Martin Luther King said, "In the end, we will remember not the words of our enemies, but the silence of our friends."

Barack Obama's Multiracial Heritage

Barack Hussein Obama Jr. was born at Kapi'olani Medical Center in Honolulu, Hawaii, on August 4, 1961. . . . Obama's father . . . was a Kenyan exchange student [who] . . . met [Obama's] mother, . . . white American Ann Dunham, when both were students at the University of Hawaii. . . . The marriage between Obama's parents dissolved in 1964, and three years later Ann Dunham married another foreign graduate student, Indonesian graduate student Lolo Soetoro. . . .

The family moved to Jakarta, Indonesia, . . . [where they enrolled Barack in a Catholic school and then in a] public but elite [elementary school]. . . . The student body there was predominantly Muslim, but Obama recalled that he did not take religious instruction at either school very seriously. . . . When Obama was ten, he was sent to Hawaii to live with his maternal grandparents. . . . Obama . . . struggled with his mixed-race identity and experimented with drugs. Even so, he . . . graduated with honors from Punahou [prep school] in 1979.

Obama attended Occidental College in Los Angeles for one year, but . . . transferred to Columbia University in New York. . . . [There he] became more aware of the American racial divide. . . . "I began to grasp the almost mathematical precision with which America's race and class problems joined, . . ." Obama recalled in his autobiography, *Dreams from My Father*. He graduated from Columbia in 1983 with a political science major and a concentration in international relations.

"Barack Obama,"
Encyclopedia of World Biography Supplement,
*vol. 32. Copyright © 2012 Cengage Learning.
All rights reserved. Reproduced by permission.*

My parents had four children during the 1950s and '60s, and thankfully we were raised in Southern California, a region more liberal and tolerant of interracial marriage than many other parts of the country.

A visceral account of the confused cultural identity I experienced in a Japanese-Jewish household can be summed up in the following quotes, the first from a Japanese emperor, "Generally speaking, the way of the warrior is the resolute acceptance of death," and the second from Woody Allen, "It's not that I'm afraid to die; I just don't want to be there when it happens."

At least as a writer, my life experiences give me more material to work with than my mother's hundreds of antique kimonos combined with all the chuppahs [a canopy used at a Jewish wedding] this side of the Golden Gate Bridge.

A perfect example of conflicting philosophies learned during childhood includes Buddha's lesson that "Life as we know it ultimately leads to suffering," while we were told simultaneously that although Jesus was indeed a suffering member of our tribe, we should never actually worship him.

But nevertheless, I have made it, I have arrived, and I am as they say in Yiddish, . . . "Nisht geferlech," which basically means "Not so shabby."

Surely President Obama must realize this profound effect he has had on a nation who soldier so many different religions, races and cultures while speaking in native tongues more freely understood now at least now in spirit, if not yet comprehended in each syllable, syntax or inflection.

A Broader and Brighter Light

And because we now have a president with a different story than presidents past, who holds his head high with his own proud blend of integral cultural being, each language and culture that is different is now more highly revered, as is each person's individual journey.

Each story sheds an even broader and brighter light on a nation that not only endures but empowers, not only inspires but includes, and not only validates, but values each lesson, paragraph and infinitesimal anecdote that boasts the value of us all.

This is now an axiomatic concept for the country, one that is only beginning to change America's story and each person willing to tell their cultural rhythms on their own.

For this one Japanese-Jewish woman who always thought she was strange; even once given the title of "Shikseh Princess" at a Bar Mitzvah by some nice Jewish boys, my story has now changed for the better and interestingly enough, still interesting all the same.

Finally I can stop commiserating with Woody Allen when he said, "My one regret in life is that I am not someone else." Except those rare moments when I begin to doubt the integrity and veracity of my own personal story that is just as valuable as anyone else's.

In his book, *The Audacity of Hope*, Obama wrote, "This is the true genius of America, a faith in the simple dreams of its people, the insistence on small miracles. That we can say what we think; write what we think, without hearing a sudden knock on the door."

The doors for us all now open with greater ease and determination, and the answers and questions we hear on the other sides of each door are purely reflective of a nation that is now more unified in its diversity, and more open to discussion, depth, profundity and inclusion.

> "When President Obama addressed the tragedy of Trayvon Martin, he demonstrated integration's great limitation—that acceptance depends not just on being twice as good but on being half as black."

Barack Obama's Presidency Has Illuminated America's Ongoing Racism

Ta-Nehisi Coates

Ta-Nehisi Coates is a senior editor at the Atlantic. *In the following viewpoint, he argues that Barack Obama managed to attain the presidency by downplaying his blackness. He says that racism and white supremacy have been central to American politics and remain a potent force. Coates agrees that Obama's election shows the extent to which racism has retreated in America, but he also points out ongoing racism. He says that muting black identity and downplaying the oppressive history, and oppressive present, of racism is the price Obama has paid for integration and provisional acceptance.*

As you read, consider the following questions:

1. According to Coates, how and why did the Trayvon Martin case become politicized?

Ta-Nehisi Coates, "Fear of a Black President," *The Atlantic*, September 2012. Reproduced by permission.

2. Coates says racism is not a simplistic hatred but is instead what?

3. What did Seth Stephens-Davidowitz do to study racial animus in the presidential election of 2008?

The irony of President Barack Obama is best captured in his comments on the death of Trayvon Martin, and the ensuing fray. Obama has pitched his presidency as a monument to moderation. He peppers his speeches with nods to ideas originally held by conservatives. He routinely cites [former Republican president] Ronald Reagan. He effusively praises the enduring wisdom of the American people, and believes that the height of insight lies in the town square. Despite his sloganeering for change and progress, Obama is a conservative revolutionary, and nowhere is his conservative character revealed more than in the very sphere where he holds singular gravity—race.

Obama and Trayvon Martin

Part of that conservatism about race has been reflected in his reticence: for most of his term in office, Obama has declined to talk about the ways in which race complicates the American present and, in particular, his own presidency. But then, last February [2012], George Zimmerman, a 28-year-old insurance underwriter, shot and killed a black teenager, Trayvon Martin, in Sanford, Florida. Zimmerman, armed with a 9 mm handgun, believed himself to be tracking the movements of a possible intruder. The possible intruder turned out to be a boy in a hoodie, bearing nothing but candy and iced tea. The local authorities at first declined to make an arrest, citing Zimmerman's claim of self-defense. Protests exploded nationally. Skittles and Arizona Iced Tea assumed totemic power. Celebrities—the actor Jamie Foxx, the former Michigan governor Jennifer Granholm, members of the Miami Heat—were photographed wearing hoodies. When Representative Bobby Rush

of Chicago took to the House floor to denounce racial profiling, he was removed from the chamber after donning a hoodie
mid-speech.

The reaction to the tragedy was, at first, trans-partisan.
Conservatives either said nothing or offered tepid support for
a full investigation—and in fact it was the Republican governor of Florida, Rick Scott, who appointed the special prosecu-
tor who ultimately charged Zimmerman with second-degree
murder. As civil rights activists descended on Florida, *National
Review*, a magazine that once opposed integration, ran a column proclaiming "Al Sharpton [a civil rights activist] Is Right."
The belief that a young man should be able to go to the store
for Skittles and an iced tea and not be killed by a
neighborhood-watch patroller seemed un-controversial.

By the time reporters began asking the White House for
comment, the president likely had already given the matter
considerable thought. Obama is not simply America's first
black president—he is the first president who could credibly
teach a black-studies class. He is fully versed in the works of
Richard Wright and James Baldwin [important twentieth century African American authors], Frederick Douglass [a leading
abolitionist in the 1800s] and Malcolm X [a civil rights leader
in the 1960s]. Obama's two autobiographies are deeply concerned with race, and in front of black audiences he is apt to
cite important but obscure political figures such as George
Henry White, who served from 1897 to 1901 and was the last
African American congressman to be elected from the South
until 1970. But with just a few notable exceptions, the president had, for the first three years of his presidency, strenu-
ously avoided talk of race. And yet, when Trayvon Martin
died, talk Obama did:

> When I think about this boy, I think about my own kids,
> and I think every parent in America should be able to un-
> derstand why it is absolutely imperative that we investigate

every aspect of this, and that everybody pulls together—federal, state, and local—to figure out exactly how this tragedy happened. . . .

But my main message is to the parents of Trayvon Martin. If I had a son, he'd look like Trayvon. I think they are right to expect that all of us as Americans are going to take this with the seriousness it deserves, and that we're going to get to the bottom of exactly what happened.

Political Fodder

The moment Obama spoke, the case of Trayvon Martin passed out of its national-mourning phase and lapsed into something darker and more familiar—racialized political fodder. The illusion of consensus crumbled. [Conservative radio talk-show host] Rush Limbaugh denounced Obama's claim of empathy. The Daily Caller, a conservative Web site, broadcast all of Martin's tweets, the most loutish of which revealed him to have committed the unpardonable sin of speaking like a 17-year-old boy. A white-supremacist site called Stormfront produced a photo of Martin with pants sagging, flipping the bird. *Business Insider* posted the photograph and took it down without apology when it was revealed to be a fake.

[Republican politician and speaker of the House of Representatives from 1995 to 1999] Newt Gingrich pounced on Obama's comments: "Is the president suggesting that if it had been a white who had been shot, that would be okay because it wouldn't look like him?" Reverting to form, *National Review* decided the real problem was that we were interested in the deaths of black youths only when nonblacks pulled the trigger. John Derbyshire, writing for *Taki's Magazine*, an iconoclastic libertarian publication, composed a racist advice column for his children inspired by the Martin affair. (Among Derbyshire's tips: never help black people in any kind of distress; avoid large gatherings of black people; cultivate black friends to shield yourself from charges of racism.)

The notion that Zimmerman might be the real victim began seeping out into the country, aided by PR [public relations] efforts by his family and legal team, as well as by various acts of stupidity—Spike Lee tweeting Zimmerman's address (an act made all the more repugnant by the fact that he had the wrong Zimmerman), NBC misleadingly editing a tape of Zimmerman's phone conversation with a police dispatcher to make Zimmerman seem to be racially profiling Martin. In April [2012], when Zimmerman set up a Web site to collect donations for his defense, he raised more than $200,000 in two weeks, before his lawyer asked that he close the site and launched a new, independently managed legal-defense fund. Although the trial date has yet to be set, as of July the fund was still raking in up to $1,000 in donations daily.

But it would be wrong to attribute the burgeoning support for Zimmerman to the blunders of Spike Lee or an NBC producer. Before President Obama spoke, the death of Trayvon Martin was generally regarded as a national tragedy. After Obama spoke, Martin became material for an Internet vendor flogging paper gun-range targets that mimicked his hoodie and his bag of Skittles. (The vendor sold out within a week.) Before the president spoke, George Zimmerman was arguably the most reviled man in America. After the president spoke, Zimmerman became the patron saint of those who believe that an apt history of racism begins with Tawana Brawley and ends with the Duke lacrosse team.[1]

I Am Trayvon Martin

The irony of Barack Obama is this: he has become the most successful black politician in American history by avoiding the radioactive racial issues of yesteryear, by being "clean" (as

---

1. Tawana Brawley was a black woman who accused six white men of raping her in 1987; the charges were dismissed. In 2006 three white members of the Duke lacrosse team were accused of raping a black woman. The charges were found to be false.

[Vice President] Joe Biden once labeled him)—and yet his indelible blackness irradiates everything he touches. This irony is rooted in the greater ironies of the country he leads. For most of American history, our political system was premised on two conflicting facts—one, an oft-stated love of democracy; the other, an undemocratic white supremacy inscribed at every level of government. In warring against that paradox, African Americans have historically been restricted to the realm of protest and agitation. But when President Barack Obama pledged to "get to the bottom of exactly what happened," he was not protesting or agitating. He was not appealing to federal power—he was employing it. The power was black—and, in certain quarters, was received as such.

No amount of rhetorical moderation could change this. It did not matter that the president addressed himself to "every parent in America." His insistence that "everybody [pull] together" was irrelevant. It meant nothing that he declined to cast aspersions on the investigating authorities, or to speculate on events. Even the fact that Obama expressed his own connection to Martin in the quietest way imaginable—"If I had a son, he'd look like Trayvon"—would not mollify his opposition. It is, after all, one thing to hear "I am Trayvon Martin" from the usual placard-waving rabble-rousers. Hearing it from the commander of the greatest military machine in human history is another.

By virtue of his background—the son of a black man and a white woman, someone who grew up in multiethnic communities around the world—Obama has enjoyed a distinctive vantage point on race relations in America. Beyond that, he has displayed enviable dexterity at navigating between black and white America, and at finding a language that speaks to a critical mass in both communities. He emerged into national view at the Democratic National Convention in 2004, with a speech heralding a nation uncolored by old prejudices and shameful history. There was no talk of the effects of racism.

Instead Obama stressed the power of parenting, and condemned those who would say that a black child carrying a book was "acting white." He cast himself as the child of a father from Kenya and a mother from Kansas and asserted, "In no other country on Earth is my story even possible." When, as a senator, he was asked if the response to Hurricane Katrina [that devastated New Orleans in 2005] evidenced racism, Obama responded by calling the "ineptitude" of the response "color-blind."

Racism is not merely a simplistic hatred. It is, more often, broad sympathy toward some and broader skepticism toward others. Black America ever lives under that skeptical eye. Hence the old admonishments to be "twice as good." Hence the need for a special "talk" administered to black boys about how to be extra careful when relating to the police. And hence Barack Obama's insisting that there was no racial component to Katrina's effects; that name-calling among children somehow has the same import as one of the oldest guiding principles of American policy—white supremacy. The election of an African American to our highest political office was alleged to demonstrate a triumph of integration. But when President Obama addressed the tragedy of Trayvon Martin, he demonstrated integration's great limitation—that acceptance depends not just on being twice as good but on being half as black. And even then, full acceptance is still withheld. The larger effects of this withholding constrict Obama's presidential potential in areas affected tangentially—or seemingly not at all—by race. Meanwhile, across the country, the community in which Obama is rooted sees this fraudulent equality, and quietly seethes.

A Man Who Happens to Be Black

Obama's first term has coincided with a strategy of massive resistance on the part of his Republican opposition in the House, and a record number of filibuster threats [whereby a minority presents a vote on a bill] in the Senate. It would be nice if this were merely a reaction to Obama's politics or his policies—if this resistance truly were, as it is generally described, merely one more sign of our growing "polarization" as a nation. But the greatest abiding challenge to Obama's national political standing has always rested on the existential fact that if he had a son, he'd look like Trayvon Martin. As a candidate, Barack Obama understood this.

"The thing is, a *black man* can't be president in America, given the racial aversion and history that's still out there," Cornell Belcher, a pollster for Obama, told the journalist Gwen Ifill after the 2008 election. "However, an extraordinary, gifted, and talented young man who happens to be black can be president."

Belcher's formulation grants the power of antiblack racism, and proposes to defeat it by not acknowledging it. His is the perfect statement of the Obama era, a time marked by a revolution that must never announce itself, by a democracy that must never acknowledge the weight of race, even while being shaped by it. Barack Obama governs a nation enlightened enough to send an African American to the White House, but not enlightened enough to accept a black man as its president.

Before Barack Obama, the "black president" lived in the African American imagination as a kind of cosmic joke, a phantom of all that could never be. White folks, whatever their talk of freedom and liberty, would not allow a black president. They could not tolerate Emmett's boyish gaze. Dr. [Martin Luther] King turned the other cheek, and they blew it off. White folks shot [President Abraham] Lincoln over "n----- equality," ran Ida Wells out of Memphis, beat Freedom Riders over bus seats, slaughtered Medgar in his driveway like a dog.[2]

---

2. Emmett Till was a fourteen-year-old boy murdered in Mississippi in 1955 for speaking to a white woman. Ida Wells was an antilynching activist in the late 1800s and early 1900s. Medgar Evers was a civil rights activist in Mississippi assassinated in 1963.

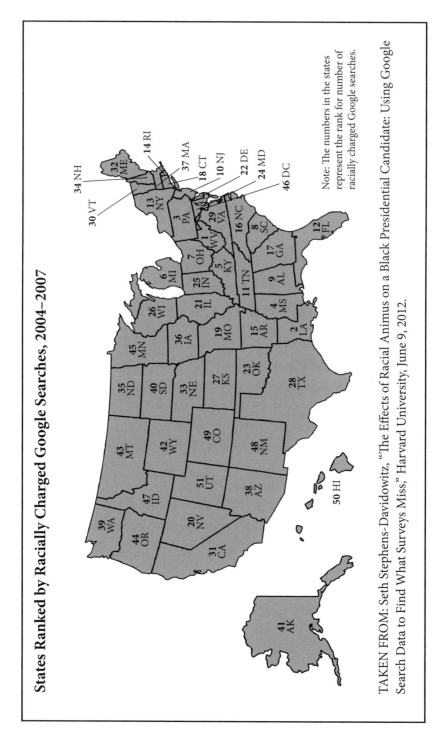

States Ranked by Racially Charged Google Searches, 2004–2007

Note: The numbers in the states represent the rank for number of racially charged Google searches.

TAKEN FROM: Seth Stephens-Davidowitz, "The Effects of Racial Animus on a Black Presidential Candidate: Using Google Search Data to Find What Surveys Miss," Harvard University, June 9, 2012.

The comedian Dave Chappelle joked that the first black president would need a "Vice President Santiago"—because the only thing that would ensure his life in the White House was a Hispanic president-in-waiting. A black president signing a bill into law might as well sign his own death certificate. . . .

The End of Racism

Watching Obama rack up victories in states like Virginia, New Mexico, Ohio, and North Carolina on Election Night in 2008, anyone could easily conclude that racism, as a national force, had been defeated. The thought should not be easily dismissed: Obama's victory demonstrates the incredible distance this country has traveled. . . . That a country that once took whiteness as the foundation of citizenship would elect a black president is a victory. But to view this victory as racism's defeat is to forget the precise terms on which it was secured, and to ignore the quaking ground beneath Obama's feet.

During the 2008 primary, the *New Yorker*'s George Packer journeyed to Kentucky and was shocked by the brazen declarations of white identity. "I think he would put too many minorities in positions over the white race," one voter told Packer. "That's my opinion." That voter was hardly alone. In 2010, Michael Tesler, a political scientist at Brown University, and David [O.] Sears, a professor of psychology and political science at UCLA [University of California, Los Angeles], were able to assess the impact of race in the 2008 primary by comparing data from two 2008 campaign and election studies with previous surveys of racial resentment and voter choice. As they wrote in *Obama's Race: The 2008 Election and the Dream of a Post-Racial America*:

> No other factor, in fact, came close to dividing the Democratic primary electorate as powerfully as their feelings about African Americans. The impact of racial attitudes on individual vote decisions . . . was so strong that it appears to

have even outstripped the substantive impact of racial attitudes on Jesse Jackson's more racially charged campaign for the nomination in 1988.

Seth Stephens-Davidowitz, a doctoral candidate in economics at Harvard, is studying how racial animus may have cost Obama votes in 2008. First, Stephens-Davidowitz ranked areas of the country according to how often people there typed racist search terms into Google. (The areas with the highest rates of racially charged search terms were West Virginia, western Pennsylvania, eastern Ohio, upstate New York, and southern Mississippi.) Then he compared Obama's voting results in those areas with John Kerry's four years earlier. So, for instance, in 2004 Kerry received 50 percent of the vote in the media markets of both Denver and Wheeling (which straddles the Ohio–West Virginia border). Based on the Democratic groundswell in 2008, Obama should have received about 57 percent of the popular vote in both regions. But that's not what happened. In the Denver area, which had one of the nation's lowest rates of racially charged Google searching, Obama received the predicted 57 percent. But in Wheeling, which had a high rate of racially charged Google searching, Obama's share of the popular vote was only 48 percent. Of course, Obama also picked up some votes because he is black. But, aggregating his findings nationally, Stephens-Davidowitz has concluded that Obama lost between 3 and 5 percentage points of the popular vote to racism.

After Obama won, the longed for post-racial moment did not arrive; on the contrary, racism intensified. At rallies for the nascent Tea Party [a right-wing Republican Party faction], people held signs saying things like Obama Plans White Slavery. Steve King, an Iowa congressman and Tea Party favorite, complained that Obama "favors the black person." In 2009, Rush Limbaugh, bard of white decline, called Obama's presidency a time when "the white kids now get beat up, with the black kids cheering 'Yeah, right on, right on, right on.' And of course everybody says the white kid deserved it—he was born a racist, he's white." On *Fox & Friends*, [conservative media personality] Glenn Beck asserted that Obama had exposed himself as a guy "who has a deep-seated hatred for white people or the white culture. . . . This guy is, I believe, a racist." Beck later said he was wrong to call Obama a racist. That same week he also called the president's health care plan "reparations" [referring to arguments that blacks should receive reparations for slavery].

One possible retort to this pattern of racial paranoia is to cite the [President Bill] Clinton years, when an ideological fever drove the right wing to derangement, inspiring militia movements and accusations that the president had conspired to murder his own lawyer, Vince Foster. The upshot, by this logic, is that Obama is experiencing run-of-the-mill political opposition in which race is but a minor factor among much larger ones, such as party affiliation. But the argument assumes that party affiliation itself is unconnected to race. It pretends that only [black author] Toni Morrison took note of Clinton's particular appeal to black voters. It forgets that Clinton felt compelled to attack Sister Souljah [a black rapper]. It forgets that whatever ignoble labels the right wing pinned on Clinton's health care plan, "reparations" did not rank among them.

Michael Tesler, following up on his research with David [O.] Sears on the role of race in the 2008 campaign, recently published a study assessing the impact of race on opposition to and support for health care reform. The findings are bracing. Obama's election effectively racialized white Americans' views, even of health care policy. As Tesler writes in a paper published in July in the *American Journal of Political Science*, "Racial attitudes had a significantly greater impact on health care opinions when framed as part of President Obama's plan than they had when the exact same policies were attributed to President Clinton's 1993 health care initiative."

Not American

While Beck and Limbaugh have chosen direct racial assault, others choose simply to deny that a black president actually exists. One in four Americans (and more than half of all Republicans) believe Obama was not born in this country, and thus is an illegitimate president. More than a dozen state legislatures have introduced "birther bills" demanding proof of Obama's citizenship as a condition for putting him on the 2012 ballot. Eighteen percent of Republicans believe Obama to be a Muslim. The goal of all this is to delegitimize Obama's presidency. If Obama is not truly American, then America has still never had a black president.

White resentment has not cooled as the Obama presidency has proceeded. Indeed, the GOP presidential primary race featured candidates asserting that the black family was better off under slavery (Michele Bachmann, Rick Santorum); claiming that Obama, as a black man, should oppose abortion (Santorum again); or denouncing Obama as a "food-stamp president" (Newt Gingrich).

The resentment is not confined to Republicans. Earlier this year, West Virginia gave 41 percent of the popular vote during the Democratic primary to Keith Judd, a white incarcerated felon (Judd actually defeated Obama in 10 counties). Joe Manchin, one of West Virginia's senators, and Earl Ray Tomblin, its governor, are declining to attend this year's Democratic convention, and will not commit to voting for Obama.

It is often claimed that Obama's unpopularity in coal-dependent West Virginia stems from his environmental policies. But recall that no state ranked higher on Seth Stephens-Davidowitz's racism scale than West Virginia. Moreover, Obama was unpopular in West Virginia before he became president: even at the tail end of the Democratic primaries in 2008, Hillary Clinton walloped Obama by 41 points. A fifth of West Virginia Democrats openly professed that race played a role in their vote.

What we are now witnessing is not some new and complicated expression of white racism—rather, it's the dying embers of the same old racism that once rendered the best pickings of America the exclusive province of un-blackness. Confronted by the thoroughly racialized backlash to Obama's presidency, a stranger to American politics might conclude that Obama provoked the response by relentlessly pushing an agenda of radical racial reform. Hardly. Daniel Gillion, a political scientist at the University of Pennsylvania who studies race and politics, examined the Public Papers of the Presidents, a compilation of nearly all public presidential utterances—proclamations, news conference remarks, executive orders—and found that in his first two years as president, Obama talked less about race than any other Democratic president since 1961. Obama's racial strategy has been, if anything, the opposite of radical: he declines to use his bully pulpit to address racism, using it instead to engage in the time-honored tradition of black self-hectoring, railing against the perceived failings of black culture.

His approach is not new. It is the approach of [nineteenth-century educator] Booker T. Washington, who, amid a sea of white terrorists during the era of Jim Crow, endorsed segregation and proclaimed the South to be a land of black opportunity. It is the approach of L. Douglas Wilder, who, in 1986, not long before he became Virginia's first black governor, kept his distance from Jesse Jackson and told an NAACP [National Association for the Advancement of Colored People] audience: "Yes, dear Brutus, the fault is not in our stars, but in ourselves. . . . Some blacks don't particularly care for me to say these things, to speak to values. . . . Somebody's got to. We've been too excusing." It was even, at times, the approach of Jesse Jackson himself, who railed against "the rising use of drugs, and babies making babies, and violence . . . cutting away our opportunity."

The strategy can work. Booker T.'s Tuskegee University still stands. Wilder became the first black governor in America since Reconstruction. Jackson's campaign moved the Democratic nominating process toward proportional allocation of delegates, a shift that Obama exploited in the 2008 Democratic primaries by staying competitive enough in big states to rack up delegates even where he was losing, and rolling up huge vote margins (and delegate-count victories) in smaller ones.

And yet what are we to make of an integration premised, first, on the entire black community's emulating the Huxtables [the upper-middle-class African American family portrayed in the 1980s sitcom "The Cosby Show"]? An equality that requires blacks to be twice as good is not equality—it's a double standard. That double standard haunts and constrains the Obama presidency, warning him away from candor about America's sordid birthmark.

> *"By 2020—just eight years away—non-white voters should rise from a quarter of the 2008 electorate to one-third. In 30 years, nonwhites will outnumber whites."*

The Republican Party Faces Marginalization as America Becomes More Multiracial

Jonathan Chait

Jonathan Chait is a writer and blogger for New York Magazine. *In the following viewpoint, he argues that the American electorate is increasingly diverse and that this diversity is on the way to creating a long-term Democratic majority. Republicans, he says, have long based their electoral coalition on white resentment of blacks and Hispanics. As these groups become a larger proportion of the electorate, Chait declares, Republicans' chance at winning declines. Chait says that Republicans have resisted adapting to the new electorate, a strategy that he contends will only damage them further in the long term.*

Jonathan Chait, "Why 2012 Is the Republicans Last Chance," *New York Magazine*, February 26, 2012. Reproduced by permission.

As you read, consider the following questions:

1. By how much does Chait say the nonwhite proportion of the electorate grows each year, and what conclusions does he draw from this?

2. What did Stanley Greenberg conclude about Reagan Democrats, as cited in the viewpoint?

3. What does Chait say was the most surprising response to the election of 2008?

Of the various expressions of right-wing hysteria that have flowered over the past three years [2009–2012]—. . . perhaps the strain that has taken deepest root within mainstream Republican circles is the terror that the achievements of the [Barack] Obama administration may be irreversible, and that the time remaining to stop permanent nightfall is dwindling away.

Demographic End

"America is approaching a 'tipping point' beyond which the Nation will be unable to change course," announces the dark, old-timey preamble to [Congressman] Paul Ryan's "The Roadmap Plan," a statement of fiscal principles that shaped the budget outline approved last spring by 98 percent of the House Republican caucus. [Former senator and 2012 candidate for the Republican presidential nomination] Rick Santorum warns his audiences, "We are reaching a tipping point, folks, when those who pay are the minority and those who receive are the majority." Even such a sober figure as [2012 Republican presidential candidate] Mitt Romney regularly says things like "We are only inches away from no longer being a free economy," and that this election "could be our last chance."

The Republican Party is in the grips of many fever dreams. But this is not one of them. To be sure, the apocalyptic *ideological* analysis—that "freedom" is incompatible with [President Bill] Clinton-era tax rates and Massachusetts-style health care—is pure crazy. But the panicked *strategic* analysis, and the sense of urgency it gives rise to, is actually quite sound. The modern GOP—the party of [Richard] Nixon, [Ronald] Reagan, and both [George] Bushes—is staring down its own demographic extinction. Right-wing warnings of impending tyranny express, in hyperbolic form, well-grounded dread: that conservative America will soon come to be dominated, in a semipermanent fashion, by an ascendant Democratic coalition hostile to its outlook and interests. And this impending doom has colored the party's frantic, fearful response to the Obama presidency.

The GOP has reason to be scared. Obama's election was the vindication of a prediction made several years before by journalist John [B.] Judis and political scientist Ruy Teixeira in their 2002 book, *The Emerging Democratic Majority*. Despite the fact that George W. Bush then occupied the White House, Judis and Teixeira argued that demographic and political trends were converging in such a way as to form a natural-majority coalition for Democrats.

The Republican Party had increasingly found itself confined to white voters, especially those lacking a college degree and rural whites who, as Obama awkwardly put it in 2008, tend to "cling to guns or religion." Meanwhile, the Democrats had increased their standing among whites with graduate degrees, particularly the growing share of secular whites, and remained dominant among racial minorities. As a whole, Judis and Teixeira noted, the electorate was growing both somewhat better educated and dramatically less white, making every successive election less favorable for the GOP. And the trends were even more striking in some key swing states. Judis and Teixeira highlighted Colorado, Nevada, and Arizona, with skyrocketing Latino populations, and Virginia and North Carolina, with their influx of college-educated whites, as the most fertile grounds for the expanding Democratic base.

Obama's victory carried out the blueprint. Campaign reporters cast the election as a triumph of Obama's inspirational message and cutting-edge organization, but above all his sweeping win reflected simple demography. Every year, the nonwhite proportion of the electorate grows by about half a percentage point—meaning that in every presidential election, the minority share of the vote increases by 2 percent, a huge amount in a closely divided country. One measure of how thoroughly the electorate had changed by the time of Obama's election was that, if college-educated whites, working-class whites, and minorities had cast the same proportion of the votes in 1988 as they did in 2008, Michael Dukakis [the Democratic presidential candidate who lost to George H.W. Bush] would have, just barely, won. By 2020—just eight years away—nonwhite voters should rise from a quarter of the 2008 electorate to one-third. In 30 years, nonwhites will outnumber whites.

The Democratic Majority and Race

Now, there are two points to keep in mind about the emerging Democratic majority. The first is that no coalition is permanent. One party can build a majority, but eventually the minority learns to adapt to an altered landscape, and parity returns. In 1969, Kevin [P.] Phillips, then an obscure Nixon-administration staffer, wrote *The Emerging Republican Majority*, arguing that Republicans could undo FDR's [Franklin D. Roosevelt's] New Deal coalition by exploiting urban strife, the unpopularity of welfare, and the civil rights struggle to pull blue-collar whites into a new conservative bloc. The result was the modern GOP. Bill Clinton [in 1992] appropriated some elements of this conservative coalition by rehabilitating his party's image on welfare and crime (though he had a little help from [third-party candidate] Ross Perot, too). But it wasn't until Obama was elected that a Democratic president could claim to be the leader of a true majority party.

The second point is that short-term shocks, like war, recession, or scandal, can exert a far more powerful influence than a long-term trend: The Watergate scandal [in which Republican president Richard Nixon was found to be engaged in numerous illegal activities], for instance, interrupted the Republican majority at its zenith, helping elect a huge raft of Democratic congressmen in 1974, followed two years later by Jimmy Carter.

But the dominant fact of the new Democratic majority is that it has begun to overturn the racial dynamics that have governed American politics for five decades. Whatever its abstract intellectual roots, conservatism has since at least the sixties drawn its political strength by appealing to heartland identity politics. In 1985, Stanley Greenberg, then a political scientist, immersed himself in Macomb County, a blue-collar Detroit suburb where whites had abandoned the Democratic Party in droves. He found that the Reagan Democrats [that is, Democrats who voted for Ronald Reagan] there understood politics almost entirely in racial terms, translating any Democratic appeal to economic justice as taking their money to subsidize the black underclass. And it didn't end with the Reagan era. Piles of recent studies have found that voters often conflate "social" and "economic" issues. What social scientists delicately call "ethnocentrism" and "racial resentment" and "ingroup solidarity" are defining attributes of conservative voting behavior, and help organize a familiar if not necessarily rational coalition of ideological interests. Doctrines like neoconservative foreign policy, supply-side economics, and climate skepticism may bear little connection to each other at the level of abstract thought.[1] But boiled down to political sound bites and served up to the voters, they blend into an indistinguishable stew of racial, religious, cultural, and nationalistic identity.

1. Neoconservatism calls for an aggressive foreign policy; supply-side economics says that cutting taxes on the wealthy will improve the economy; climate skepticism denies global warming.

Obama's election dramatized the degree to which this long-standing political dynamic had been flipped on its head. In the aftermath of George McGovern's 1972 defeat, neoconservative intellectual Jeane Kirkpatrick disdainfully identified his voters as "intellectuals enamored with righteousness and possibility, college students, for whom perfectionism is an occupational hazard; portions of the upper classes freed from concern with economic self-interest," and so on, curiously neglecting to include racial minorities. All of them were, in essence, people who heard a term like "real American" and understood that in some way it did not apply to them. Today, cosmopolitan liberals may still feel like an embattled sect—they certainly describe their political fights in those terms—but time has transformed their rump minority into a collective majority. As conservative strategists will tell you, there are now more of "them" than "us." What's more, the disparity will continue to grow indefinitely. Obama actually lost the over-45-year-old vote in 2008, gaining his entire victory margin from younger voters—more racially diverse, better educated, less religious, and more socially and economically liberal.

Portents of this future were surely rendered all the more vivid by the startling reality that the man presiding over the new majority just happened to be, himself, young, urban, hip, and black. When jubilant supporters of Obama gathered in Grant Park on Election Night in 2008, Republicans saw a glimpse of their own political mortality. And a galvanizing picture of just what their new rulers would look like.

Strike Now

In the cold calculus of game theory, the expected response to this state of affairs would be to accommodate yourself to the growing strength of the opposing coalition—to persuade pockets of voters on the Democratic margins they might be better served by Republicans. Yet the psychology of decline does not always operate in a straightforward, rational way. A strategy of managing slow decay is unpleasant, and history is replete with instances of leaders who persuaded themselves of the opposite of the obvious conclusion. Rather than adjust themselves to their slowly weakening position, they chose instead to stage a decisive confrontation. If the terms of the fight grow more unfavorable with every passing year, well, all the more reason to have the fight sooner. This was the thought process of the antebellum Southern states, sizing up the growing population and industrial might of the North. It was the thinking of the leaders of Austria-Hungary [before World War I], watching their empire deteriorate and deciding they needed a decisive war with Serbia to save themselves.

At varying levels of conscious and subconscious thought, this is also the reasoning that has driven Republicans in the Obama era. Surveying the landscape, they have concluded that they must strike quickly and decisively at the opposition before all hope is lost.

Arthur [C.] Brooks, the president of the conservative American Enterprise Institute [for Public Policy Research] and a high-profile presence on the Republican intellectual scene, wrote a 2010 book titled *The Battle*, urging conservatives to treat the struggle for economic libertarianism as a "culture war" between capitalism and socialism, in which compromise was impossible. Time was running short, Brooks pleaded in apocalyptic tones. The "real core" of what he called Obama's socialistic supporters was voters under 30. "It is the future of our country," he wrote. "And this group has exhibited a frightening openness to statism in the age of Obama."

The same panic courses through a new tome by James De-Mint, who has made himself probably the most influential member of the Senate by relentlessly pushing his colleagues to the right and organizing primary challenges to snuff out any hint of moderation among his co-partisans. DeMint's book, titled *Now or Never*, paints a haunting picture: "Republican supporters will continue to decrease every year as more Americans become dependent on the government. Dependent voters will naturally elect even big-government progressives who will continue to smother economic growth and spend America deeper into debt. The 2012 election may be the last opportunity for Republicans."

That apocalyptic rhetoric is just as common among voters as among conservative eggheads and party elites. Theda Skocpol, a Harvard sociologist, conducted a detailed study of Tea Party activists and discovered that they saw themselves beset by parasitic Democrats. "Along with illegal immigrants," she wrote, "low-income Americans and young people loom large as illegitimate consumers of public benefits and services."

It's easy for liberals to dismiss these fears as simple racism—and surely racism, to some degree, sways the Tea Party. But it is not just conservative white people who react fearfully when they see themselves outnumbered by an influx of people unlike themselves. Minorities do it. White hipsters do it. Recall the embarrassing spectacle of liberal panic, in the aftermath of George W. Bush's reelection, when [Democratic candidate in the 2004 election John] Kerry voters believed their country had been taken over by gay-bashing Evangelical Christians.

That the struggles over the economic policies of the last few years have taken on the style of a culture war should come as no surprise, since conservatives believe Obama has pulled together an ascendant coalition of voters intent on expropriating their money. Paul Ryan, the House Republican budget chairman, has, like many Republicans, cast the fight as pitting "makers" against "takers," with the latter in danger of irrevocably gaining the upper hand. "The tipping point represents two dangers," he announced in a speech at the American Enterprise Institute, "first, long-term economic decline as the number of makers diminishes [and] the number of takers grows. . . . Second, gradual moral-political decline as dependency and passivity weaken the nation's character."

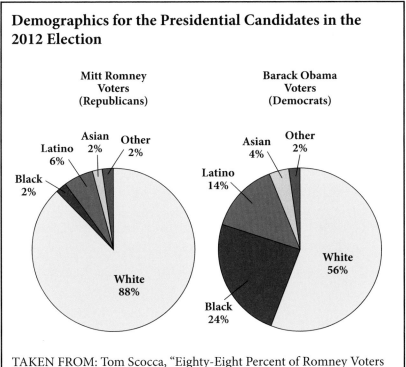

Demographics for the Presidential Candidates in the 2012 Election

Mitt Romney
Voters
(Republicans)

Latino 6%
Asian 2%
Other 2%
Black 2%
White 88%

Barack Obama
Voters
(Democrats)

Asian 4%
Other 2%
Latino 14%
White 56%
Black 24%

TAKEN FROM: Tom Scocca, "Eighty-Eight Percent of Romney Voters Were White," *Slate*, November 7, 2012.

The Hispanic Vote

Of course, both parties make use of end-times rhetoric, especially in election season. What's novel about the current spate of Republican millennialism is that it's not a mere rhetorical device to rally the faithful, nor even simply an expression of free-floating terror, but the premise of an electoral strategy.

In that light, the most surprising response to the election of 2008 is what did not happen. Following Obama's win, all sorts of loose talk concerning the Republican predicament filled the air. How would the party recast itself? Where would it move left, how would it find common ground with Obama, what new constituencies would it court?

The most widely agreed-upon component of any such undertaking was a concerted effort to win back the Hispanic vote. It seemed like a pure political no-brainer, a vital out-reach to an exploding electoral segment that could conceivably be weaned from its Democratic leanings, as had previous generations of Irish and Italian immigrants, without altering the party's general right-wing thrust on other issues. George W. Bush had tried to cobble together a comprehensive immigration-reform policy only to see it collapse underneath a conservative grassroots revolt, and John McCain, who had initially co-sponsored a bill in the Senate, had to withdraw his support for it in his pursuit of the 2008 nomination.

In the wake of his defeat, strategists like Karl Rove and Mike Murphy urged the GOP to abandon its stubborn opposition to reform. Instead, incredibly, the party adopted a more hawkish position, with Republicans in Congress rejecting even quarter-loaf compromises like the DREAM Act [acronym for Development, Relief, and Education for Alien Minors, a bill to allow some immigrants, such as those who came to the United States as small children, to become citizens] and state-level officials like [Arizona governor] Jan Brewer launching new restrictionist crusades. This was, as Thomas [Byrne] Edsall writes in *The Age of Austerity*, "a major gamble that the GOP can continue to win as a white party despite the growing strength of the minority vote."

None of this is to say that Republicans ignored the rising tide of younger and browner voters that swamped them at the polls in 2008. Instead they set about keeping as many of them from the polls as possible. The bulk of the campaign has taken the form of throwing up an endless series of tedious bureaucratic impediments to voting in many states—ending same-day voter registration, imposing onerous requirements upon voter-registration drives, and upon voters themselves. "Voting liberal, that's what kids do," overshared William O'Brien, the New Hampshire House speaker, who had supported a bill to prohibit college students from voting from their school addresses. What can these desperate, rearguard tactics accomplish? They can make the electorate a bit older, whiter, and less poor. They can, perhaps, buy the Republicans some time.

And to what end? The Republicans' most audacious choice is the hyperaggressive position they've adopted against Obama to sabotage his chances for a second term. Frustrated liberals, assessing the methods of the Republicans in Congress, see a devious brilliance at work in the GOP strategy of legislative obstruction. And indeed, Republicans very skillfully ground the legislative gears to a halt for months on end, weakening or killing large chunks of Obama's agenda, and nurturing public discontent with Washington that they rode to a sweeping victory in 2010. At the same time, their inability to waver from desperate, all-or-nothing opposition often meant conservatives willingly suffered policy defeats for perceived political gain, and failed to minimize the scale of those defeats.

No Compromise

Take the fight over health care reform. Yes, Republicans played the politics about as well as possible. But it was their hard line on compromise [that] allowed the bill to pass: The Democrats only managed to cobble together 60 votes to pass it in the Senate because conservatives drove [Pennsylvania senator] Arlen Specter out of the GOP, forcing him to switch to the Democratic Party. Without him, Democrats never could have broken a filibuster. When Scott Brown surprisingly won the 2010 race to fill Ted Kennedy's Senate seat, Democrats were utterly despondent, and many proposed abandoning comprehensive health care reform to cut a deal for some meager expansion of children's health insurance. But Republicans refused to offer even an olive branch. Presented with a choice between passing the comprehensive bill they had spent a year cobbling together or collapsing in total ignominious defeat, the Democrats passed the bill.

Last summer, Obama was again desperate to reach compromise, this time on legislation to reduce the budget deficit, which had come to dominate the political agenda and symbolize, in the eyes of establishment opinion, Obama's failure to fulfill his campaign goal of winning bipartisan cooperation. In extended closed-door negotiations, Obama offered Republicans hundreds of billions of dollars in spending cuts and a permanent extension of Bush-era tax rates in return for just $800 billion in higher revenue over a decade. This was less than half the new revenue proposed by the Bowles-Simpson deficit commission [officially known as the National Commission on Fiscal Responsibility and Reform]. Republicans spurned this deal, too.

Instead the party has bet everything on 2012, preferring a Hail Mary strategy to the slow march of legislative progress. That is the basis of the House Republicans' otherwise inexplicable choice to vote last spring for a sweeping budget plan that would lock in low taxes, slash spending, and transform Medicare into private vouchers—none of which was popular with voters. Majority parties are known to hold unpopular votes occasionally, but holding an unpopular vote that Republicans knew full well stood zero chance of enactment (with Obama casting a certain veto) broke new ground in the realm of foolhardiness.

The way to make sense of that foolhardiness is that the party has decided to bet everything on its one "last chance." Not the last chance for the Republican Party to win power—there will be many of those, and over time it will surely learn to compete for nonwhite voters—but its last chance to exercise power in its current form, as a party of antigovernment fundamentalism powered by sublimated white Christian identity politics. (And the last chance to stop the policy steamroller of the new Democratic majority.) And whatever rhetorical concessions to moderates and independents the eventual Republican nominee may be tempted to make in the fall, he'll find himself fairly boxed in by everything he's already done this winter [during the 2012 primaries] to please that base.

Gambling on Depression

Will the gamble work? Grim though the long-term demography may be, it became apparent to Republicans almost immediately after Obama took office that political fate had handed them an impossibly lucky opportunity. Democrats had come to power almost concurrently with the deepest economic crisis in 80 years, and Republicans quickly seized the tactical advantage, in an effort to leverage the crisis to rewrite their own political fortunes. The Lesser Depression could be an economic Watergate, the Republicans understood, an exogenous political shock that would, at least temporarily, overwhelm any deeper trend, and possibly afford the party a chance to permanently associate the Democrats with the painful aftermath of the crisis.

During the last midterm elections, the strategy succeeded brilliantly. Republicans moved further right and won a gigantic victory. In the 2010 electorate, the proportion of voters under 30 fell by roughly a third, while the proportion of voters over 65 years old rose by a similar amount—the white share, too. In the long run, though, the GOP has done nothing at all to rehabilitate its deep unpopularity with the public as a whole, and has only further poisoned its standing with Hispanics. But by forswearing compromise, it opened the door to a single shot. The Republicans have gained the House and stand poised to win control of the Senate. If they can claw out a presidential win and hold on to Congress, they will have a glorious two-year window to restore the America they knew and loved, to lock in transformational change, or at least to wrench the status quo so far rightward that it will take Democrats a generation to wrench it back. The cost of any foregone legislative compromises on health care or the deficit would be trivial compared to the enormous gains available to a party in control of all three federal branches.

On the other hand, if they lose their bid to unseat Obama, they will have mortgaged their future for nothing at all. And over the last several months, it has appeared increasingly likely that the party's great all-or-nothing bet may land, ultimately, on nothing. In which case, the Republicans will have turned an unfavorable outlook into a truly bleak one in a fit of panic. The deepest effect of Obama's election upon the Republicans' psyche has been to make them truly fear, for the first time since before Ronald Reagan, that the future is against them.

"*[The Republican Party] clearly wanted to be perceived as embracing a multiracial future. The question is: Were voters convinced?*"

The Republican Party Is Trying to Promote Multiracial Leaders

Christine A. Scheller

Christine A. Scheller is a writer and editor at Explorations Media. In the following viewpoint, she examines the racial politics of the 2012 Republican National Convention. She reports that there were not many African American delegates to the convention but says that the Republican Party worked to include diverse speakers, such as former secretary of state Condoleezza Rice and New Mexico governor Susana Martinez. Scheller also singles out several convention speeches that focused on minority issues and policies. She concludes that the Republicans are trying to appear inclusive, though she is not convinced that their efforts will sway many minority voters.

As you read, consider the following questions:

1. What does Scheller say was the high point of the convention among speakers of color, and on what basis does she make this claim?

2. What policies were touted by Jeb Bush at the convention, according to Scheller?

3. Who is BeBe Winans, and what role does Scheller say he played at the convention?

The stage of the Republican National Convention that concluded in Tampa last night [in August 2012] was a lot more colorful than the floor, at least when it came to skin color. . . . With speeches by African Americans, Indian Americans, and Hispanic Americans, one might have thought the GOP was the party of color. But, Baratunde Thurston, author of *How to Be Black*, was in Tampa reporting for WNYC and Yahoo! News, and decided to count how many black people were actually in attendance. He curated his count under the Twitter hashtag #negrospotting. (That apparently got conservative firebrand Michelle Malkin fired up.) His last count, reported this morning, was 238 African Americans among the 5,000+ attendees.

Condoleezza Rice, Artur Davis, and Jeb Bush

The high point among speakers of color, at least according to an unscientific survey of my journalist-heavy Twitter feed, was former secretary of state Condoleezza Rice, who gave a hard-hitting foreign policy speech Wednesday night. Even those who didn't care for the substance of Rice's speech conceded that her delivery was impressive, perhaps even presidential. "When the world looks to America, they look to us because we are the most successful political and economic experiment in human history. That is the true basis of 'American Exceptionalism,'" said Rice. "The essence of America—that which really unites us—is not ethnicity, or nationality or religion—it is an idea—and what an idea it is: That you can come from humble circumstances and do great things."

Former Democratic representative from Alabama Artur Davis said we should have known better than to have been seduced by the hype surrounding Barack Obama back in 2008. "Do you know why so many of us believed?" said the former Obama supporter. "We led with our hearts and our dreams that we could be more inclusive than America had ever been, and no candidate had ever spoken so beautifully. But dreams meet daybreak: the jobless know what I mean, so do the families who wonder how this administration could wreck a recovery for three years and counting. So many of those high-flown words have faded."

Jeb Bush, the one-time Florida governor whose wife is Mexican American, defended his brother George W. Bush's record and talked passionately about educating children of color. "We need to set high standards for students and teachers and provide students and their parents the choices they deserve. The first step is a simple one. We must stop prejudging children based on their race, ethnicity or household income," said Bush. He then highlighted what he said are Florida's achievements in improving academic performance, particularly for students of color. "Here in Florida in 1999, we were at the bottom of the nation in education. For the last decade, this state has been on a path of reform," he said. Among African-American students, Florida is ranked fourth in the nation for academic improvement, among low-income students, the state is third, among students with disabilities, it is first, and, among Latino students, "the gains were so big, they required a new metric," Bush said.

Susana Martinez, Mia Love, and Nikki Haley

New Mexico governor and former Democrat Susana Martinez delivered a rousing speech noting her own ethnic "first." "As the first Hispanic female governor in history, little girls often come up to me in the grocery store or the mall. They look and point, and when they get the courage, they ask 'Are you Susana?' and they run up and give me a hug," said Martinez. "It's in moments like these when I'm reminded that we each pave a path. And for me, it's about paving a path for those little girls to follow. No more barriers."

Up-and-coming U.S. congressional candidate and mayor of Saratoga Springs, Utah, Mia Love called President Obama's version of America "a divided one—pitting us against each other based on our income level, gender, and social status." She said the story of the American Dream is one "of human struggle" that has "been told for over 200 years with small steps and giant leaps; from a woman on a bus to a man with a dream; and the bravery of the greatest generation, to the entrepreneurs of today." Love, like Mitt Romney, is also a Mormon.

South Carolina governor Nikki Haley defended her state's controversial immigration law, calling it "innovative." Said Haley, "We said in South Carolina that if you have to show a picture ID to buy Sudafed and you have to show a picture ID to set foot on an airplane, then you should have to show a picture ID to protect one of the most valuable, most central, most sacred rights we are blessed with in America—the right to vote. And what happened? President Obama stopped us."

Racial Diversity?

On the convention floor, meanwhile, a couple delegates made headlines for throwing peanuts at a black CNN camerawoman and saying, "This is what we feed animals." Patricia Carroll, the camerawoman, was reticent about the incident, telling *Journal-isms* [a blog] it could have happened anywhere, including the Democratic convention, but she was not surprised it happened in Tampa. "This is Florida, and I'm from the

Deep South," she said. "You come to places like this, you can count the black people on your hand. They see us doing things they don't think I should do."

Even PBS's news anchors seemed to enjoy gospel singer BeBe Winans's stirring rendition of "America America." Winans, who performed on the final night, told *Essence* magazine that he saw his reportedly unpaid participation in the convention as a display of bipartisanship. He was not unaware of how controversial it would be for him to sing there, he said. "The RNC [Republican National Committee] realized this was something that could work to their advantage and I realized there is a master plan here," remarked Winans. "And so my message to them and to the world is that we are all Americans before we are a part of any political party. It's so simple and yet we make it so difficult."

True. But, of course, by definition political conventions are neither the time nor place for bipartisanship. Rather, they are an occasion for creating a narrative for what each party believes America should truly be. And this party clearly wanted to be perceived as embracing a multiracial future. The questions is: Were voters convinced?

Oh, and in case you were wondering, former Massachusetts governor Mitt Romney accepted the Republican nomination for president and Wisconsin congressman Paul Ryan agreed to be his VP, if the people so choose.

Update 9/2: Baratunde Thurston clarified his post: "The final final count is in, and I spotted 238 Negroes during the RNC [Republican National Convention], 239 if I count seeing my own reflection in various mirrors and windows. I estimated no more than 60 of those to be authenticated GOP delegates or party members. It turns out the actual number of black delegates was 46."

Periodical and Internet Sources Bibliography

The following articles have been selected to supplement the diverse views presented in this chapter.

Ta-Nehisi Coates	"The Latino Vote: Wide Awake, Cranky, Taking Names," *Atlantic*, November 7, 2012.
Conor Friedersdorf	"The GOP Must Choose: Rush Limbaugh or Minority Voters," *Atlantic*, November 9, 2012.
Cord Jefferson	"Commentary: Morgan Freeman's Misguided 'Mixed-Race President' Quote," BET, July 9, 2012.
Alexandra Le Tellier	"Obama's Reelection Bid: Has Obama Alienated 9 Million Multiracial Voters?," *Los Angeles Times*, April 4, 2011.
Kevin Nobel Maillard	"Playing the Interracial Card," *Campaign Stops* (blog), *New York Times*, July 12, 2012. http://campaignstops.blogs.nytimes.com.
Andrea Stone	"Multiracial American Population Grew Faster than Single-Race Segment in 2010 Census," *Huffington Post*, September 27, 2012. www.huffingtonpost.com.
Seth Freed Wessler	"Is This the End of the Southern Strategy, or Its Entrenchment?," Colorlines, November 12, 2012. http://colorlines.com.
Edward Wyckoff Williams	"The Multiracial Face of the Democratic Party," The Root, November 13, 2012. www.theroot.com.
Clinton Yates	"Barack Obama: Let's Not Forget That He's America's First Bi-racial President," *The Root DC* (blog), *Washington Post*, November 8, 2012. www.washingtonpost.com/blogs/therootdc.

OPPOSING
VIEWPOINTS®
SERIES

CHAPTER 2

How Can Multiracial America Become More Equal?

Chapter Preface

In 1954 the Supreme Court ruled that states could not pass laws segregating schools. The landmark decision in *Brown v. Board of Education*, which declared that separate school systems for white and black students were never and could never be equal, was one of the most important civil rights court decisions in US history, and it was vital to dismantling America's system of segregation and racial oppression.

Despite its importance, however, many schools remained segregated years after the *Brown* decision. According to a February 8, 2007, article at ACLU.org, in that year, one in six black children and one in ten Latino children attended schools that had 90 percent or more students of color. In a May 19, 2012, article in the *New York Times*, David L. Kirp said that desegregation was effectively dead as a national policy, as a new conservative Supreme Court had ruled against various desegregation schemes.

Kirp argues that the abandonment of integration is justified on the grounds that the real problem in schools is not segregation but poor teaching. Kirp insists that "a spate of research says otherwise." He adds:

> The experience of an integrated education made all the difference in the lives of black children—and in the lives of their children as well. These economists' studies consistently conclude that African-American students who attended integrated schools fared better academically than those left behind in segregated schools. They were more likely to graduate from high school and attend and graduate from college; and, the longer they spent attending integrated schools, the better they did. What's more, the fear that white children would suffer, voiced by opponents of integration, proved groundless. Between 1970 and 1990, the black-white gap in

educational attainment shrank—not because white young-sters did worse but because black youngsters did better.

Laura McKenna, writing in a May 21, 2012, guest post on Megan McArdle's *Atlantic* blog, agrees that integration may have helped some minority students. But she emphasizes that the forced integration of the 1970s, in which students were bused to more distant schools to create more diverse class-rooms, is neither feasible nor desirable. She says that parents resist such integration not because they are racist, but because they are self-interested:

> It's a natural parental drive to provide your kids with the best things in life—a nice home, good food and an excellent education, even if it comes at the expense of others or it flies in the face of political ideology. Our last two Demo-cratic presidents sent their children to private schools, while at the same time having lunch with the teachers' unions. Parents want their kids in the Gifted and Talented Programs and don't want the special education kids to suck up too many resources.

> While there's little evidence that a diverse student body in terms of income, ethnicity, or cognitive abilities creates a worse learning environment for the most privileged kids, any threat to a child drives a parent insane. Protecting one's child is a natural instinct, and school reformers must deal with this instinct with compassion.

McKenna says that because of the strong emotions in-volved, integration should be pursued cautiously, slowly, and sympathetically.

The viewpoints in this chapter look further at segregation and other issues of equality and fairness in multiracial America.

│ *"Our argument is that you need affir-*
│ *mative action to make meritocratic de-*
│ *cisions—to get the best candidates."*

Affirmative Action Is Needed to Get the Best Candidates, Stanford Psychologist Says

Brooke Donald

Brooke Donald is a former Associated Press reporter who currently writes for the Stanford News. *In the following viewpoint, she discusses research by psychologist Greg Walton about affirmative action. Walton argues that because of discrimination, minority groups often perform worse on standardized tests than their ability indicates. Therefore, to get the best candidates, Walton argues, schools may need to use affirmative action to offset the discrepancy in test scores. Walton concludes that affirmative action may be necessary to ensure merit-based admissions.*

As you read, consider the following questions:

1. What is *Fisher v. University of Texas*, according to the viewpoint?

2. What is stereotype threat, and how does it affect performance, according to the viewpoint?

3. Besides affirmative action, what other remedies does Walton suggest?

The researchers plan to submit their findings to the U.S. supreme Court, which is expected to hear arguments next fall on what could become a landmark affirmative action case.

When it comes to affirmative action, the argument usually focuses on diversity. Promoting diversity, the Supreme Court ruled in 2003, can justify taking race into account.

But some people say this leads to the admission of less qualified candidates over better ones and creates a devil's choice between diversity and merit.

Not so, says Stanford psychologist Greg Walton. Diversity and meritocracy are not always at odds.

In fact, sometimes it is only by taking race and gender into account that schools and employers can admit and hire the best candidates, Walton argues in a paper slated for publication in the journal *Social Issues and Policy Review* with coauthors Steven J. Spencer of the University of Waterloo and Sam Erman of Harvard University.

Walton, an assistant professor of psychology, and Spencer plan to present their findings to the Supreme Court in an amicus brief in *Fisher v. University of Texas*, a case the justices are scheduled to hear next fall and that many court watchers believe threatens to upend affirmative action. (Supreme Court rules bar Erman, who was a recent Supreme Court clerk, from participating in the brief.)

"People have argued that affirmative action is consistent or is not consistent with meritocracy," Walton said. "Our argument is not that it's consistent or inconsistent. Our argument is that you need affirmative action to make meritocratic decisions—to get the best candidates."

The researchers say that people often assume that measures of merit like grades and test scores are unbiased—that they reflect the same level of ability and potential for all students.

Under this assumption, when an ethnic-minority student and a non-minority student have the same high school grades, they probably have the same level of ability and are likely to do equally well in college. When a woman and a man have the same score on a math test, it's assumed they have the same level of math ability.

The problem is that common school and testing environments create a different psychological experience for different students. This systematically disadvantages negatively stereotyped ethnic minority students like African Americans and Hispanic Americans, as well as girls and women in math and science.

"When people perform in standard school settings, they are often aware of negative stereotypes about their group," Walton says. "Those stereotypes act like a psychological headwind—they cause people to perform worse. If you base your evaluation of candidates just on performance in settings that are biased, you end up discriminating."

The conclusion comes out of research on what is called stereotype threat—the worry people have when they risk confirming a negative stereotype about their group. That worry prevents people from performing as well as they can, hundreds of studies have found.

As a consequence, Walton says, "Grades and test scores assessed in standard school settings underestimate the intellectual ability of students from negatively stereotyped groups and their potential to perform well in future settings."

Walton gives an example of how stereotype threat relates to preferences in admissions or hiring.

A woman and a man each apply to an elite engineering program, he says. The man has slightly better SAT math scores than the woman. He gets accepted to the program, but she does not.

"If stereotype threat on the SAT undermined the woman's performance and as a consequence caused her SAT score to

Preferential Treatment for Whites

Whiteness, as I was coming to learn, is about never being really out of place, of having the sense that wherever you are, you belong. . . . Despite my lousy test scores and mediocre grades, no one ever thought to suggest that I had somehow gotten into Tulane because of "preferential treament," . . . Students of color, though, with even better grades and scores, had to regularly contend with this sort of thing, since they were presumed to be the less-qualified beneficiaries of affirmative action. But what kind of affirmative action had *I* enjoyed? What preference had I received? Of course it wasn't race directly. It's not as if Tulane had admitted me *because* I was white. Clearly, my admission was related to having been on one of the top debate teams in the nation, but that wasn't even a talent that I'd be putting to use in college, so why had it mattered? And my academic credentials *had* been overlooked. . . .

Nowadays, I lecture around the country in defense of affirmative action and meet plenty of whites who resent the so-called lowering of standards for students of color but swallow without comment the lowering of standards for the children of alumni. . . . Studies indicate there are twice as many whites who fail to meet normal admission standards but who are admitted anyway thanks to "connection preferences" as there are persons of color who receive any consideration from affirmative action. Yet rarely do the critics of affirmative action seem to mind this form of preferential treatment.

Tim Wise, White Like Me:
Reflections on Race from a Privileged Son.
Berkeley, CA: Soft Skull Press, 2008.

underestimate her potential, then by not taking that bias into account, you have effectively discriminated against the woman," Walton says.

Walton and his colleagues argue that schools need to take affirmative steps to level the playing field and to make meritocratic decisions. If the SAT underestimates women's math ability or the ability of African American students, taking this into account will help schools both admit better candidates and more diverse ones.

While courts have ruled that diversity justifies taking race into account in admissions decisions, justices have not considered meritocracy as a reason for sorting by race.

"Our argument is that it is only by considering race that you can make meritocratic decisions," Walton says. "It's a separate argument from the diversity argument."

Walton's research provides the justices with another reason for upholding affirmative action.

But confronting legal questions is only part of the issue.

Walton says remedies need to be found in policy, as well. Environments need to be created that are fair and allow people to do well.

"The first step is for organizations to fix their own houses," he says.

Testing officials should look at how they administer tests and ask what they can do to mitigate the psychological threats that are present in their settings that cause people to do poorly, Walton says.

Schools and employers, he continues, should look into their own internal environments and ask how they can make those environments safe and secure so everyone can do well and stereotypes are off the table.

But if stereotype threat was present in a prior environment, hiring and admissions decisions need to take that into account.

"In taking affirmative steps," Walton, Spencer and Erman write, "organizations can promote meritocracy and diversity at once."

> "Accepting an affirmative action leg up probably hurts a student's chances of becoming a doctor, scientist or engineer."

Affirmative Action Does Not Help Minority Students

Gail Heriot

Gail Heriot is a professor of law at the University of San Diego and a member of the US Commission on Civil Rights. In the following viewpoint, she says that studies have shown that affirmative action hurts minority students who major in science and engineering. She says that students who get an affirmative action placement in more difficult schools are often discouraged from pursuing science and engineering. On the other hand, she notes, students who attend schools in line with their abilities are more likely to complete science and engineering degrees. She concludes that affirmative action policies should be reconsidered.

As you read, consider the following questions:

1. According to Heriot, are college-bound African Americans more or less likely to express a desire to pursue a major in science or engineering?

Gail Heriot, "Opinion: Does Affirmative Action Help College Students?," AOL News, December 24, 2010. Copyright © 2010 AOL Inc. Used with permission.

2. What evidence does Heriot provide that the discouraging effects of affirmative action are significant?

3. How successful have historically black colleges and universities been in graduating engineering and science majors, according to Heriot?

All across the country, high school seniors are gearing up to apply to college. Many of them assume that the best thing they can do to ensure a bright future is to attend the most prestigious school that has accepted them—even if their race, athletic prowess or rich uncle helped them get in.

Affirmative Action Hurts Scientists

But according to a December [2010] report of the U.S. Commission on Civil Rights, that may be a mistaken strategy—at least for students hoping for a degree in science or engineering.

The extensive research compiled in that report concludes that accepting an affirmative action leg up probably hurts a student's chances of becoming a doctor, scientist or engineer. A better strategy is to attend a school at which one's entering academic credentials roughly match the median student's.

Contrary to some people's expectations, college-bound African-Americans express a desire to major in science and engineering as often as whites and maybe a little more often. But something happens during college, and they disproportionately abandon that ambition, taking up softer majors instead. By graduation, African-Americans are markedly under-represented in science and engineering bachelor's degrees—a gateway credential for many well-paying, prestigious careers.

For decades, some blamed the attrition problem wholly on African-Americans' science-related standardized test scores, which remain on average lower than those of whites or Asians. It should surprise no one to learn that students with lower standardized test scores are indeed less likely to stick with science and engineering than students with higher scores, no matter where they attend school.

But that's not the whole story.

As three independent scholarly studies show, part of the problem appears to be relative. A student who attends a college at which his entering credentials put him near the bottom of the class—which is where a student who needed an affirmative action preference will be—is less likely to persevere in science or engineering than an otherwise identical student attending a school at which those same credentials put him in the middle of the class or higher.

Discouraged

The reasons for this comparative effect are doubtless complex. But they are based on a common everyday observation: A good student can get in over his head and end up learning little or nothing if he is placed in a classroom with students whose level of academic preparation is much higher than his own, even though he is fully capable of mastering the material when presented at a more moderate pace. Discouraged, he may even give up—even though he would have persevered and ultimately succeeded in a somewhat less competitive environment.

The effect does not appear to be slight. In a 2004 article, University of Virginia psychology professor Frederick Smyth and University of Southern California psychology professor John McArdle predicted that 45 percent more minority women and 35 percent more minority men in their sample would have persisted in science and engineering if they had attended schools where their academic credentials matched their peers.

Further proof of the inadvertent harm being caused by affirmative action can be found in the remarkable success of historically black colleges and universities [HBCUs], where half of African-American students naturally have entering credentials in the top half of the class.

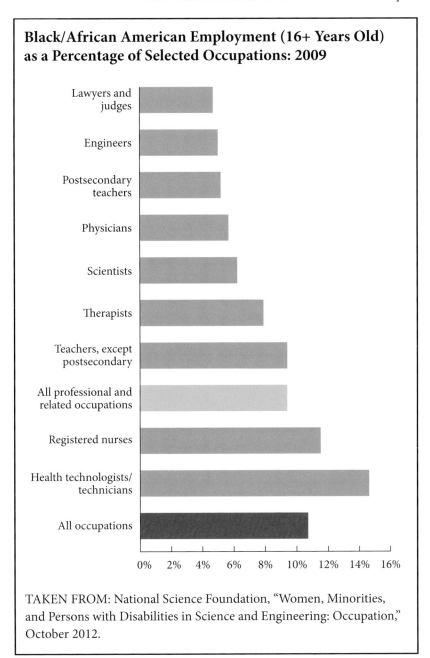

Black/African American Employment (16+ Years Old) as a Percentage of Selected Occupations: 2009

TAKEN FROM: National Science Foundation, "Women, Minorities, and Persons with Disabilities in Science and Engineering: Occupation," October 2012.

HBCUs graduate more than their proportionate share of African-American students with science and engineering degrees and send more than their share on to get PhDs at mainstream institutions. A few years back, for example, the National Science Foundation reported that with only 20 percent of total African-American enrollment, HBCUs produce 40 percent of the African-Americans graduating with a bachelor's degree in the natural sciences. This is impressive.

All of this is something high school seniors deserve to know. The commission challenges colleges and universities to tell them.

| *"Asian Americans are the new Jews, in-
heriting the mantle of the most disenfranchised group in college admissions."*

Asian Americans Complicate the Argument for Affirmative Action

Richard Kahlenberg

*Richard Kahlenberg is a senior fellow at the Century Foundation
and the author of* The Remedy: Class, Race and Affirmative
Action. *In the following viewpoint, he reports that some Indian
American and other Asian groups have started to oppose affirmative action. He argues that in many cases Asian American
representation in schools increases when affirmative action is
lifted. Asian Americans are often considered to be overrepre-
sented in admissions, he says, and so have to get higher test
scores than other groups. Since Asian Americans have suffered
from discrimination in the past, he says, the fact that they are
hurt by affirmative action calls the policy's rationale into question.*

As you read, consider the following questions:

1. What evidence of past discrimination against Asian Americans does Kahlenberg discuss?

Richard Kahlenberg, "Asian Americans and Affirmative Action," *The Chronicle of Higher
Education*, June 1, 2012. Copyright © 2012 by Richard Kahlenberg. All rights reserved.
Reproduced by permission.

2. What differences in Asian American enrollment are there between Berkeley and Princeton, and what factors might account for this difference?

3. What is the difference between "floors" and "ceilings" for admissions, according to Kahlenberg?

The amicus briefs for those challenging affirmative-action policies at the University of Texas were due to the Supreme Court earlier this week [in June 2012], and among the most talked about are those filed by Asian-American groups. Traditionally, most Asian-American organizations have supported affirmative action, but as Peter Schmidt notes in the *Chronicle*, the decision of three major Indian-American organizations to oppose affirmative-action policies this week "reflects a marked departure from the position most other Asian-American groups have taken on the issue." The Indian-American groups joined the Asian American Legal Foundation, which has long opposed affirmative action, in filing amicus briefs calling for an end to racial preferences.

Hurting Victims of Discrimination

The increasing split within the Asian-American community is awkward for supporters of affirmative action because the case of Asian Americans highlights two significant vulnerabilities of racial-preferences programs.

First, the treatment of Asian Americans under diversity policies underlines the tension between the historic "remedial" notion of affirmative action (that we should seek to compensate victims of discrimination) and the reality that affirmative-action policies today sometimes penalize members of groups who were historically victims of discrimination.

While Asian Americans were not the subject of slavery in America, Japanese Americans were interned during World War II, and Chinese Americans have been subjected to segregation. The Asian American Legal Foundation brief notes that "Asian-

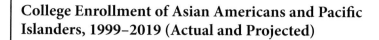

College Enrollment of Asian Americans and Pacific Islanders, 1999–2019 (Actual and Projected)

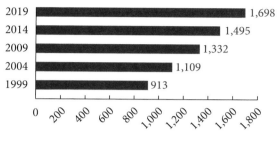

Note: Actual data, 1999–2009; projected data, 2014 and 2019.
Source: U.S. Department of Education, Common Core Data;
U.S. Department of Education, IPEDS.

TAKEN FROM: Beth Richter, "30 Percent Increase Projected for Asian American and Pacific Islander Undergraduates," Noel-Levitz, October 26, 2011.

American schoolchildren were some of the first victims of the separate-but-equal doctrine endorsed in *Plessy v. Ferguson*" [an 1896 Supreme Court decision that legalized segregation].

Yet race-conscious policies appear to significantly damage the prospect of Asian-American applicants today. When affirmative action was banned in California in 1996, the brief from Indian-American groups notes, Asian freshman enrollment at UC [the University of California at] Berkeley soared from 37.3 percent in 1995 to 46.6 percent in 2005. According to a study by Thomas Espenshade and Chang Chung of Princeton University, eliminating racial preferences of all types would increase Asian-American admission at several elite universities studied from 23.7 percent to 31.5 percent.

Likewise, Columbia University's Andrew Delbanco points out in his new book, *College: What It Was, Is, and Should Be*, that at Berkeley, where grades and test scores count overwhelmingly, Asian-American students now make up almost 50 percent of the student body, while at Princeton, where "personal qualities" figure into the mix, Asians constitute less than 20 percent of the class. Even accounting for the fact that California is more heavily Asian (13 percent) than the rest of the country (around 5 percent), the discrepancy between the two institutions is "striking," Delbanco writes.

Under-Representation, Over-Representation

Second, the emphasis of affirmative action on group representation, and "under-representation" in the case of African Americans and Latinos, raises issues of what to do about "over-representation" of groups like Asian Americans. It is true, as supporters of affirmative action argue, that one can draw a principled distinction between "floors" (ensuring groups have minimal representation) and "ceilings" (capping the representation of certain groups.) But, in practice, it appears that universities have come to apply both floors and ceilings, which helps explain why Asian Americans have to score 140 SAT points higher than whites to be admitted at selective institutions, according to a recent book by Espenshade and Alexandria Walton Radford. In both sets of amicus briefs, Asian-American groups draw a parallel between Jewish quotas from the early part of the twentieth century, and caps on Asian admission today in an environment where race is routinely accepted as a valid factor to be considered. Both briefs quote journalist Daniel Golden's contention that "Asian Americans are the new Jews, inheriting the mantle of the most disenfranchised group in college admissions."

As long as Asian American groups presented a mostly solid phalanx of support for affirmative action, these issues could be downplayed. But with the emergence of a split, the thorny issues posed by Asian Americans may be hard for the U.S. Supreme Court to ignore.

> "When Congress does get around to changing our immigration laws, it should consider ways of encouraging the assimilation of immigrants, as well [as] deciding on whom and how many to admit."

The United States Should Encourage Assimilation of Immigrants

Linda Chavez

Linda Chavez is an author, commentator, radio talk-show host, and author of Out of the Barrio: Toward a New Politics of Hispanic Assimilation. *In the following viewpoint, she argues that immigrants are assimilating well into American culture. She adds, however, that there is room for improvement, and she recommends that federal policies should be designed to encourage assimilation. Specifically, she argues that the government should give preferential status to immigrants who learn English and to those who wish to enter the military.*

As you read, consider the following questions:

1. What does Chavez say is good news about today's immigrants?

2. Why does Chavez say that it is no wonder that Mexicans have the lowest civic assimilation rates?

3. How does Chavez suggest the United States might encourage English speaking among immigrants?

A new study out this week [mid-May 2008] by the Manhattan Institute [for Policy Research] should dispel a few myths on immigrant assimilation.

Immigrants and the American Mainstream

The study looked at a range of factors—economic, cultural, and civic—to assess whether today's immigrants are becoming part of the American mainstream.

But it also compared this generation of immigrants to the Great Wave who came to America's shores in the early part of the 20th century.

The good news is that today's immigrants appear to be assimilating at faster rates than those older generations of immigrants, even though they start out with more disadvantages.

Not surprisingly, some immigrant groups—Canadians, Cubans and Filipinos—are perfectly assimilated on economic measures, while others, especially Mexicans, lag behind.

The study's author, Duke University professor Jacob L. Vigdor, looked at earned income, labor force participation, unemployment, occupation, educational attainment and home ownership in computing economic assimilation.

On these measures Canadian, Cuban, and Filipino immigrants were indistinguishable from the native born.

But the study also contained some interesting surprises. For example, Vietnamese immigrants scored 99 (on a scale of 100) on economic assimilation and exhibited the highest degree of civic assimilation (as measured by naturalization rates and military service).

However, they scored about the same on cultural assimilation (as measured by English proficiency, intermarriage, and childbearing) as Mexicans and Salvadorans.

And the groups that fared the worst on cultural assimilation measures were Indians and Chinese; while Mexicans, Salvadorans, Canadians and Indians measured poorly on civic assimilation.

The study did not distinguish between immigrants who entered the country legally and those who entered illegally, because census data don't include such information.

But, of course, across all measures, legal status is critical to assimilation.

Mexicans are far more likely than other immigrants to have entered the U.S. illegally, so it's no wonder they have the lowest civic assimilation rates and fare more poorly on economic measures.

But, what about Canadian and Indian immigrants? There's little clue why they don't join the military or become citizens at higher rates.

Vigdor does suggest that those who scored highest on civic assimilation, Vietnamese and Filipinos, come from countries that experienced recent U.S. military intervention in the past 100 years.

But so did the Dominican Republic, whose immigrants score in the middle range on civic assimilation.

The immigration debate—at least at the national level—has simmered down since its boiling point last summer.

Confused Immigration Policy

Congress continues to abrogate its responsibility to come up with reasonable immigration reform, but it can't avoid doing so forever. States and local jurisdictions already have tried to fill the void, but with mixed—you might say schizophrenic—results.

Steps in Assimilation

The early writings about the process of assimilation in America necessarily focused on the pull of the American culture. Anglo conformity was a requirement for moving up in the emergent American space. However, "unlearning" one's culture or identity is a severe proposition. Immigrants do not "unlearn" their culture or their identity as they become assimilated; rather they go through stages of integration and then take on attributes that do not unmake their identities, but remake them. The stages of assimilation (the final phase of immigrant incorporation) have been described as follows:

1. Acculturation: cultural or behavioral assimilation or the adoption of customs and language

2. Structural assimilation: entry into cliques, clubs and institutions

3. Marital assimilation: intermarriage

4. Identification assimilation: development of new identities

5. Attitude reception assimilation: decrease and eventual absence of prejudice

6. Behavioral reception assimilation: decrease and eventual absence of discrimination

7. Civic assimilation: decrease and eventual absence of conflict

Yoku Shaw-Taylor,
Immigration, Assimilation, and Border Security.
Lanham, MD: Government Institutes, 2012, p. 63.

Arizona, for example, passed tough laws to punish employers who hire illegal immigrants, only to find itself in a labor crunch, with dire consequences for the state economy.

Now Arizona, Colorado, and a handful of other states are exploring whether they can create their own "guest worker" programs to bring in more Mexican workers.

When Congress does get around to changing our immigration laws, it should consider ways of encouraging the assimilation of immigrants, as well [as] deciding on whom and how many to admit.

We should give priority to immigrants who already speak English, since this is a key factor in their successful integration into American society.

That doesn't mean we take only people who hail from English-speaking countries; language is, after all, a skill that can be learned.

But why not give incentives for learning English before they get their green card?

And why not encourage employers who want to hire these workers by giving them tax incentives if they offer on-the-job English classes to improve immigrants' skills?

We also could give priority admission to immigrants willing to serve in the U.S. military, provided they have the requisite English and educational skills.

Successful assimilation should be the goal of U.S. immigration policy. Instead, it's usually given short shrift in drafting immigration laws.

When Congress takes up the issue again, as it most assuredly must next year, we should look to improving our assimilation index across all measures: economic, cultural, and civic.

| "[Immigrants] come with the baggage of their identities of the home country and often want to cling to them, the way we cling to precious heirlooms that have been handed down for generations."

Immigrants Should Not Be Pushed to Assimilate

Laura Marcus

Laura Marcus is a recruiter at Deep Springs College. In the following viewpoint, presented in a debate while she was a student at Yale University, she argues that people always have competing identities in different communities. She says that immigrants are rooted in their home cultures and home communities and that those cultures ground them and give their lives meaning. She says that immigrants are also connected to American culture and will adopt many aspects of their new home. However, she concludes, to force immigrants to give up most or all aspects of their home culture is against America's belief in self-fulfillment and happiness for all.

As you read, consider the following questions:

1. According to D'Souza's speech, what does Marcus conclude that it means to succeed?

2. What identities does Marcus list as her own?

3. Why does Marcus suggest that it is natural that immigrants are willing to adopt an American identity?

Good evening ladies and gentlemen! Regarding tonight's resolution in particular, that immigrants should assimilate, there are those here who say yea, there are those who say nay, and then there are those who say loudly and proudly: to a certain extent! I am delighted to stand before you this evening to raise high the banner for us moderates, who by necessity are often marginalized by the dichotomous structure of debate. For I am sure that I am not alone in my belief that a little assimilation is for the best. That it would be beneficial and desirable if immigrants to America should, say, follow the laws, try to develop an appreciation for civil rights, and perhaps learn a little English.

Culture and Self-Fulfillment

But I reject strongly Mr. [Dinesh] D'Souza's[1] assertion that immigrants must divest themselves of all but the superficial elements of their culture, and in this speech I propose to explain why.

Mr. D'Souza argues that immigrants should "assimilate to those strategies that will best help them to succeed." Well, what does it mean to succeed? According to Mr. D'Souza's speech, it may be one of two things: (1) material success, the value of which he himself contests or (2) some abstract self-fulfillment of the individual. He did not sketch out the latter to my satisfaction, so I will do so now.

I would contest that self-fulfillment, abstract a concept though it may be, is much, much harder to attain without a robust culture that provides structure, meaning, and purpose to our lives.

1. Dinesh D'Souza is a conservative intellectual; he spoke in favor of immigrants' assimilating at the same debate from which this viewpoint is taken.

Mr. D'Souza dismisses the importance of culture offhand, as something "rooted in the cult," and therefore, one supposes, something antiquated, superstitious, and essentially false and foolish. Flimsy as such etymological arguments are, I am pleased to rebut him on his own grounds. Culture indeed may be rooted in the cult. But humans are rooted in humus, the soil—the way we relate to it, the way we cultivate it. We are tied by nature to our own piece of soil. To sever ourselves from this piece of soil is to sever us not only from our culture, but from our humanity.

So what do we make of these transplants, immigrants? Now Mr. D'Souza has argued that two competing values systems—say, American values and so-called "old country" values—can never exist side by side. That one must necessarily be made subordinate to the other.

Well yes, they cannot be reconciled into a coherent philosophical framework, but I do not put so much stock in coherent philosophical frameworks anyway. They are at best pernicious and at worst blasphemous—freshmen, don't let them tell you otherwise!

I know many, many people in this room—and I am one of them—who struggle in vain to reconcile their identities, knowing full well that they carry with them commitments that can never be made into a perfect whole. And yet we do not rid ourselves, for convenience's sake, of one of these identities. They are part of us, and they exist side by side!

Many Identities

Now I have a lot of identities. Mi Mamá es de México, Meine Großmutter kommt aus Deutschland. . . . [2]

I'm a Hawaiian by birth, a Hoosier by upbringing, a Colts fan therefore by necessity, a woman, a Yale student, a Humanities major, and, as of about 2:45 this afternoon, a paying member of the Tango Club.

---

2. In Spanish she says, "My mother is from Mexico;" and in German, "My grandmother is from Germany."

But my two most important identities are my identity as an American and my identity as a Jew—and the commitments that these identities carry with them are very, very often at odds with one another.

America says, "all men are created equal." Judaism says, "Ye shall be holy, for I the Lord your God am holy."

America says, "egalitarianism." Judaism says, "gender roles."

America says, "cheeseburger." Judaism says, "OU certified glatt kosher beef patty with parve tofutti topping. Or cholent."

And you'd better believe that I embrace all of these dichotomies with a whole heart. It is a constant struggle to navigate a life in which I honor—to the best of my abilities—the claims made on me by these two forces, but I do not feel in any way at a loss for it. If I, in all the sincerity of my soul, treat both as they are—as inextricable aspects of my life, as commitments that make me who I am—I feel I am in no way a worse American, nor a worse Jew.

Immigrants find themselves in a similar position, though even more exacerbated by the trauma of transplantation. They come with the baggage of their identities of their home country and often want to cling to them, the way we cling to precious heirlooms that have been handed down for generations. But most times they are happy to adopt an American identity alongside it. After all, if there weren't something appealing about the American outlook, why would they have come?

And we should be content with that. To ask more would be to ask immigrants to give up a part of themselves. And in a country . . . which does hold self-fulfillment as an ideal, that should be the last thing we require of those who seek to make America their home.

Periodical and Internet Sources Bibliography

The following articles have been selected to supplement the diverse views presented in this chapter.

Ethan Bronner	"Asian Americans in the Argument," *New York Times*, November 1, 2012.
Michael Kinsley	"Affirmative Action Hurts Minorities. Really?," *News & Observer* (Raleigh, NC), September 6, 2012.
David L. Kirp	"Making Schools Work," *New York Times*, May 19, 2012.
Michaela Krauser	"Segregation Continues in Urban Schools," *Salon*, July 11, 2012.
Jillian Kay Melchior	"Asian Americans' Affirmative-Action Quandary," *The Corner* (blog), *National Review*, September 5, 2012. www.nationalreview.com /corner.
Dowell Myers and John Pitkin	"Assimilation Today," Center for American Progress, September 1, 2010. www.american progress.org.
Myron Orfield	"How the Suburbs Gave Birth to America's Most Diverse Neighborhoods," *Atlantic*, July 20, 2012.
Sam Roberts	"Segregation Curtailed in U.S. Cities, Study Finds," *New York Times*, January 30, 2012.
UPI.com	"Census: Integration of U.S. Cities Slows," December 15, 2010. www.upi.com.
Jonathan Yockey	"Column: Affirmative Action Hurts Everyone Involved," Online Gargoyle, October 21, 2011. www.uni.illinois.edu.

OPPOSING
VIEWPOINTS®
SERIES

CHAPTER 3

What Issues Surround Multiracial Relationships in America?

Chapter Preface

In an increasingly diverse America, Hawaii stands out as uniquely multiracial. It is the most ethnically diverse state in the United States. According to the US Census Bureau, as of 2011 only 26 percent of Hawaiians are white, as compared to 78 percent of the US population as a whole. The majority racial designation in Hawaii is Asian, at 38.5 percent of the population (in contrast to 5 percent nationally). Native Hawaiian and other Pacific Islanders make up another 10 percent of the population. Hispanics make up 9.2 percent—a number that has increased rapidly in recent years, though it is still significantly below the 16.7 percent national Latino population. African Americans make up about 2 percent of the population (as opposed to 13 percent nationally).

Hawaii is diverse not only in terms of groups, but in terms of individuals. In the United States as a whole, only about 2.3 percent of people identify two or more races on census forms. In Hawaii, that number is 22.9 percent, or almost one-quarter of the island's inhabitants. Among those over eighteen years old, the number of people claiming two or more races jumped by 31 percent between 2000 and 2010.

Sarah C.W. Yuan, a demographer at the University of Hawaii's Center on the Family, attributed the rapid increase in multiracial identification to a growing number and acceptance of multiracial marriages in Hawaii, according to a February 25, 2011, *USA Today* article by William M. Welch. Rates of interracial marriage are increasing throughout the country, and especially in the western United States, where a 2012 study found that fully 20 percent of marriages were between couples of different races. Those figures look paltry compared to Hawaii, however, where 40 percent of marriages between 2008 and 2010 involved couples of two different ethnic groups, as reported by Rebecca Trounson in a February 16, 2012, article for the *Star Advertiser*. Hawaii is starting to approach the point where a married couple is as likely to be of different races as not.

Though the rest of the nation is far behind Hawaii's pace, it nonetheless seems to be the case that, in terms of interracial marriage, the rest of the United States is moving in the same direction. The viewpoints in this chapter discuss the changing attitudes and issues surrounding multiracial couples and marriages.

> *"Large majorities of 18- to 29-year-olds express support for interracial marriage within their families, and the level of acceptance in this generation is greater than in other generations."*

Interracial Marriages Are Increasingly Accepted in America

Pew Research Center

The Pew Research Center is a nonpartisan fact tank that provides public opinion polling, demographic analysis, and other research. In the following viewpoint, the center reports on its recent studies showing very high rates of acceptance of interracial marriage among those eighteen to twenty-nine years old, a group that the center refers to as Millennials. It adds that older groups have also become more accepting of interracial marriage and dating over time, though older groups remain somewhat less accepting than the Millennials.

As you read, consider the following questions:

1. Among those over fifty, what differences does the author find among blacks and whites in acceptance of interracial marriage?

2. What demographic characteristics besides age does the viewpoint say are correlated with acceptance of interracial relationships?

3. What percentages of different races and age groups say they have at least some friends of different races?

Over the last several decades, the American public has grown increasingly accepting of interracial dating and marriage. This shift in opinion has been driven both by attitude change among individuals generally and by the fact that over the period, successive generations have reached adulthood with more racially liberal views than earlier generations. Millennials are no exception to this trend: Large majorities of 18- to 29-year-olds express support for interracial marriage within their families, and the level of acceptance in this generation is greater than in other generations.

Millennials Are More Accepting of Interracial Marriage

The Pew Research Center's recent report on racial attitudes in the U.S. finds that an overwhelming majority of Millennials, regardless of race, say they would be fine with a family member's marriage to someone of a different racial or ethnic group. Asked about particular groups to which they do not belong, Millennials are about equally accepting of marriage to someone in any of the groups tested: Roughly nine in ten say they would be fine with a family member's marriage to an African American (88%), a Hispanic American (91%), an Asian American (93%) or a white American (92%).

This high level of acceptance among Millennials holds true across ethnic and racial groups; there is no significant difference between white, black and Hispanic Millennials in the degree of acceptance of interracial marriage.

Compared with older groups, particularly Americans ages 50 or older, Millennials are significantly more likely to be accepting of interracial marriage. While 85% of Millennials say they would be fine with a marriage to someone from any of the groups asked about, that number drops to about three-quarters (73%) among 30- to 49-year-olds, 55% among 50 to 64-year-olds, and just 38% of those ages 65 and older. And unlike among Millennials, among those ages 50 and older there are substantial differences between blacks and whites in acceptance of interracial marriage, with older blacks considerably more accepting of interracial marriage than are whites of the same age.

The gap between Millennials and other age groups is evident for all of the individual groups asked about, though the size of the gap does vary as Americans ages 50 to 64 and 65 and older are less likely to accept marriages to members of some groups (in particular, African Americans) than others (in particular, white Americans).

Other demographic characteristics also are correlated with attitudes toward interracial marriage. Both overall and within each generation, acceptance of interracial marriage is positively associated with being female and with higher levels of education. And among older generations, those who can count at least some members of other races as friends and those who live outside of the South are also more accepting of interracial marriage.

Shift in Public Attitudes over Time

Not surprisingly, given the high levels of acceptance of interracial marriage among Millennials, nearly all 18- to 29-year-olds (93%) agree with the statement "I think it is all right for

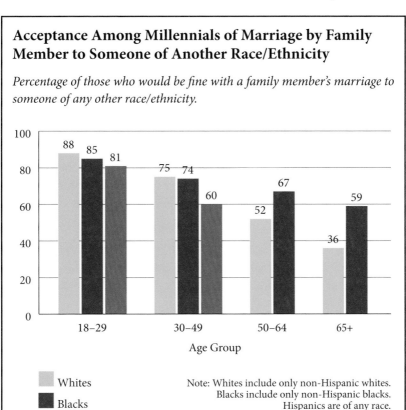

Acceptance Among Millennials of Marriage by Family Member to Someone of Another Race/Ethnicity

Percentage of those who would be fine with a family member's marriage to someone of any other race/ethnicity.

Whites
Blacks
Hispanics

Note: Whites include only non-Hispanic whites. Blacks include only non-Hispanic blacks. Hispanics are of any race. Insufficient cases of Hispanics ages 50–64 and 65+ for analysis.

TAKEN FROM: Pew Research Center, "Almost All Millennials Accept Interracial Dating and Marriage," February 1, 2010.

blacks and whites to date each other." Pew Research has tracked responses to this question for more than two decades in its study of American political values, most recently in April 2009. These surveys have found Millennials very accepting of interracial dating since the opinions of this generation first were tracked in 2003 (in 2003, 92% of Millennials agreed that it was all right for blacks and whites to date).

When the first Generation Xers began to be tracked in the late 1980s, about two-thirds of this generation (those born between 1965 and 1980) agreed that it was "all right for blacks and whites to date each other." By the time all members of that generation had reached age 18, fully 85% agreed with the statement—about the same proportion as does so today (86%). The opinions of Baby Boomers (those born between 1946 and 1964) became more accepting of black-white dating in the early 1990s and have steadily become more so; in recent years, Boomers have become almost as accepting of interracial dating as Gen Xers. The oldest generation currently being tracked, the "Silent" generation (those born between 1928 and 1946), has steadily become more racially liberal over time, though they remain significantly less likely to approve of interracial dating than are those in younger generations (68% in 2009).

In addition to their racially liberal views on marriage and dating, a majority of Millennials (54%) in Pew Research's report on race say at least some of their friends are of a different race. The percentage of white Millennials saying they have black friends (56%) is about the same as the percentage of black Millennials who say they have white friends (55%). There is little difference on this question between Millennials and Americans ages 30 to 49. But Americans ages 50 and older are considerably less likely to have cross-racial friendships, and this difference is largely the result of fewer older whites having black friends. Just 36% of whites ages 50 to 64 and 32% of whites ages 65 and older report having at least some black friends. There are no statistically significant differences between older and younger blacks in reports of cross-racial friendships.

> *"Parents of both white and black kids have a lot of anxiety about the prospect of interracial dating."*

Interracial Dating Exposes Divide Between Teens and Parents

Chuck Hadad

Chuck Hadad is a producer for the news show Anderson Cooper 360°. *In the following viewpoint, he discusses a study conducted by the news show that found that children were much more comfortable with interracial dating than were their parents. He reports that many teens say that their parents discourage interracial dating. Hadad also explains that the rate of interracial dating is rising, and he concludes by pointing out that discouraging interracial dating can have detrimental effects in terms of the likelihood of young people forming interracial friendships and their attitudes toward race and diversity.*

As you read, consider the following questions:

1. What statistics does Hadad cite to show that interracial marriage is increasing?

2. Why did Jimmy's father say that Jimmy's slew of white girlfriends concerned him?

3. What double standard does Chantay believe her family has about interracial dating?

CNN—Luke, a white seventh grader, believes his parents would not be supportive if he dated an African-American girl. "Honestly I don't think my parents would be too happy because . . . if you marry a black girl, you're connected to their family now," he said, adding, "and who knows what her family is really like?"

Jimmy, a black seventh grader, recounted that after he had several white girlfriends, his parents seemed to interpret it as an affront to his own race. "They said, 'Why not your own kind?' because all my girls have been white," he said, adding, "it's not like they were like, 'You need to choose a black girl,' it's just they were asking me why I like white girls and I was just like, 'there's no . . . specific reason.'"

Their stories highlight a divide not between the races, but between the generations. Both teens participated in an *Anderson Cooper 360°* study on children and race. Many students reported discouragement of interracial dating from their parents, or those of their friends, with reactions ranging from wariness to outright forbiddance.

The architect of the AC360° study, renowned child psychologist Dr. Melanie Killen, says parents of both white and black kids have a lot of anxiety about the prospect of interracial dating. Killen, who was hired as a consultant for the study, contends the trepidation from parents can have a profound negative effect on their children's friendships and racial attitudes as a whole.

"Parents of young children do often send messages about, 'We can all be friends . . . with everybody,' . . . but by adolescence, they start getting more nervous about this and they start thinking, 'Well you should be friends with people like you or like us,'" said Killen. She added that parents' ultimate fear is often that their children will marry another race. While interracial couples are a source of conflict for some families, interracial marriage is on the rise in America. According to a recent report by the Pew Research Center using the most recent census data, 8.4% of marriages are interracial compared to just 3.2% in 1980 and in 2010, a full 15.1% of all new marriages were interracial.

Anderson Cooper and Soledad O'Brien interviewed a panel of parents whose children participated in the AC360° study and were vocal about the issue of interracial dating. The father of Luke, the white middle schooler, said his son might have gotten the wrong impression from a conversation he and his wife had with Luke's older sister.

"She informed me she had started going out with an African-American ... young man at her school. A young man that we knew, and that we liked a lot and it wasn't that we didn't so much want them dating because of race per se. We didn't know if she had really thought about some of the cultural differences that there may be and so we talked about it in that respect ... not that it's right or wrong, good or bad, just different," said Luke's father Gary.

He also admitted that the issues facing friends in interracial marriages were at the forefront of his mind. "They have great marriages. They also have shared challenges at times. Challenges in the way the families may relate, challenges that they themselves may have either between themselves or the perception of other people ... we've talked about those kind of things because they're real," said Gary.

The father of Jimmy, the black teen, said he's supportive of his son dating girls of any race but his son's slew of white girlfriends did get him concerned. "When you see your kid always steering towards a different race, you want to make sure that he doesn't have a problem with his own race ... because we'd never seen him with a black girlfriend," said Jimmy's father, also named Jimmy.

Black Men with White Wives Discuss Their Family's Reactions to Their Marriages

One professional black husband indicated that it was difficult to separate out "race" issues from "class" issues when considering his wife's family and his own family's response to their interracial marriage. He observed that his wife comes from a rural area in the United States and from a large family in which most members are not very educated. His wife was one of the first people in her family to leave the area to go to college and later to graduate school. He felt that his wife was "light years" away in thinking and attitudes from her family and, because of her life experiences, was very strong in her belief that the marriage would work. She discounted any racial concerns her family may have had about their relationship, attributing these to the homogenous rural area in which her family resided.

One black husband contended that his mother was the person who had the most difficulty with his marriage. He was surprised by her response because his mother was not visibly distinguishable from white in her physical appearance. He believed that her concern with his choice of spouse was due to her wish that he marry a woman from his cultural and ethnic background.

Cheryl Yvette Judice,
Interracial Marriages Between Black Women and White Men.
Amherst, NY: Cambria Press, 2008, p. 107.

Another black seventh grader who participated in the study, 13-year-old Chantay, admitted she, and others in her extended family, had a double standard regarding interracial dating.

"If I were to date a white guy, a lot of people wouldn't really have a problem with that. But if my brother were to bring home a white girl, there's definitely going to be some you know controversy," she said, adding, "I think it's more of a problem for people when a black man brings home a white woman because it's been like that for years."

Chantay's mother Christal says she'd support her children dating any race but thinks her daughter's issue reveals concerns about whether black men view black women as inferior. "I think when she speaks about if her brother were to bring home a white girl, what it says I think to our kids, our black kids, is, 'Are we not good enough for our black brothers? What's wrong with us? What, do you like the silky straight hair? I can press my hair,'" said Christal.

As for the parents who spoke to Cooper and O'Brien, they said hearing their children's thoughts on interracial dating was revelatory and would spark more conversations at home. For Killen, raising these issues in parents' minds is essential because they can have unintended long-term consequences. She says perceived discouragement of interracial dating can, "contribute to more negative messages about being friends with people of different racial or ethnic backgrounds," adding, "then that sets in a whole set of expectations that could be lifelong."

> "More black women marrying out, Banks suggests in a simple calculus, would eliminate the ratio disparity between unmarried black men and women, and thus the problems his book addresses."

Marrying Out

John H. McWhorter

John H. McWhorter is a City Journal *contributing editor. In the following viewpoint, McWhorter discusses the book* Is Marriage for White People?: How the African American Marriage Decline Affects Everyone *by Ralph Richard Banks. Banks looks at the low marriage rate of black women and suggests that marrying outside the black race would help the race. McWhorter with Banks looks at a few reasons why the marriage rate of black women is low as well as several reasons why black women do not marry outside their race as much as women of other races do, which also contributes to the low marriage rate of black women. McWhorter suggests that impulses among black women to preserve the race may "constitute a tribalist comfort zone" and may be an obstacle to finding a marriage partner.*

As you read, consider the following questions:

1. On average, on a scale of 1 to 10, how many black women are unmarried in today's society? What was the marriage rate of black women in the 1950s?

2. According to the author, what races of men responded more often to black women than white men or black men did, in the OkCupid survey?

3. What are four reasons that black women give for not wanting to marry outside of their race, according to the author?

*B*lack women will have to become more open to nonblack partners, Ralph Banks argues.

Is Marriage for White People?: How the African American Marriage Decline Affects Everyone, by Ralph Richard Banks (Dutton, 304 pp., $25.95).

Stanford Law School professor Ralph Banks's *Is Marriage for White People?* is essentially about a black American interviewee he calls Audrey. She's 39, graduated from prestigious black college Spelman, and has an M.B.A. She has travelled the world and has a plush job with a multinational consulting firm. She is also unmarried and sees few signs that that will change.

What interests Banks is that Audrey is, in this last detail, typical. Seven out of ten black women are unmarried, and college-educated black women are twice as likely as their white female peers not to be married by their thirties. That is, they're no more likely to marry or stay married—black divorce rates are also twice as high as white—than white women with only a high school diploma. The picture is little better for black men, fewer than half of whom are husbands. (Affluent black men, in fact, become less likely to marry the more money they earn—the reverse of the trend for white men.) Moreover, neither Africa nor slavery is the culprit here: as late as the 1950s, nine in ten black women married.

Banks's book focuses mostly on black women, partly because their rates of singlehood are higher, partly because they were more forthcoming in interviews, and partly because he sees them as the ones who could solve the problem. "For black women, being unmarried has become the new normal, single the new black," he writes.

It's now standard to point to the high incarceration rates of black men, which render the ratio of women to available men unsuitably high, as a main cause of the black marriage crisis. But Banks focuses on educated black women, whom we would not expect this problem to affect. Audrey's singlehood owes to other factors. One is that black men "marry out" of their racial group (about one in five) more than black women do (fewer than one in ten). Asian and Latino women are over three times as likely to marry out of their group as black women.

The naive observer would simply ask why black women don't follow this lead and marry out more. Banks usefully recalls the hit film *Waiting to Exhale*, in which four black women in Phoenix are frustrated in finding love. Blacks constitute a mere 5 percent of Phoenix's population, yet the possibility of the characters' dating nonblack men is never even considered. Common wisdom also holds that white men simply aren't interested in black women. A 2009 University of California— Irvine study of Internet dating found that 90 percent of white men specifying a racial preference excluded black women, while a study of the dating site OkCupid (conducted by its operators) showed that white men write back to black women's messages 25 percent less than compatibility scores would predict.

Banks points out, however, that in the OkCupid study, Latino, Middle Eastern, Indian, and Native American men responded to black women at higher rates than white men— and often, black men—did. In the UC Irvine study, moreover, fewer than 60 percent of the white men noted any racial preference, which means that overall, half of white men expressed openness to black women. That portion of white men would add up to a larger population than that of all black men.

The Internet studies, then, haven't shown that a concealed but potent racism largely bars black women from dating other races. Some white men also told Banks that they assumed black women would reject them, and Banks argues that much of the problem is, indeed, black women's resistance to dating out. For some, the issues are elemental: some black women prefer a vernacular "swagger" more common in black men than in whites. Others can't imagine marrying someone fundamentally unlike their fathers.

Other reasons for the resistance are more political, and they raise further questions. Many black women worry that a white man's family wouldn't accept them. Yet the heartening fact is that whereas, in 1958, 94 percent of whites in one survey disapproved of interracial marriage, today, among those under 35, only 6 percent do. Black women also express a desire for black-skinned children to help preserve the race. Here, again, we might imagine hearing large numbers of Mexican or Korean-American women saying the same thing—but we don't. If the difference is that entire countries of Mexicans and Koreans exist, we might point to the widely accepted idea that black Americans are "African-American," and thereby could lay claim to an entire continent. In any case, resistance to "miscegenation" conforms to neither the American ideal, the Civil Rights vision, nor brute biological imperatives.

Still more reasons: many black women say they don't want to explain aspects of black female hair care to nonblack men. But what would we think of, say, a Korean woman who didn't want to explain the food she grew up eating to a prospective partner? Black women also complain that white partners don't "get" racism, but as Banks shows, whites' competing accounts of incidents a black partner terms "racist" are hardly always inaccurate. Not all clerks who ask "May I help you?" are troubled that you have entered their store; sometimes a funny look is just a funny look.

Banks carefully parses the point: "If fears of interracial intimacy keep people separate now, it is because those fears embody the echo of the past. Many of us continue to act out the roles we first began to inhabit long ago. We scarcely stop to consider that we might change the script." Meanwhile, black women often endure their men dating other women at the same time, a practice encouraged by the ratio problem, and shown in studies to be more common among black than white men. More black women marrying out, Banks suggests in a simple calculus, would eliminate the ratio disparity between unmarried black men and women, and thus the problems his book addresses. "For black women," Banks argues in what seems the book's money quote, "interracial marriage doesn't abandon the race, it serves the race."

Well, yes. Yet can Banks's counsel, sound as it is, make a difference in the real world—let alone change cultural predilections set since infancy for the likes of "swagger"? Banks hopes his cool, clear reasoning can educate a person out of impulses to "preserve the race." These impulses, though, often constitute a tribalist comfort zone; they form one way that a black person can gain the basic human comfort in belonging.

I'm inclined to think that the new generation of black women will be more open to nonblack partners. For now, however, Banks's book will stand as a poignant description of a generation of accomplished women who discovered that the tribalist impulse their parents fostered in them—parents for whom that impulse was a necessity—has become an obstacle to finding marriage partners in multicultural America.

> *"To imply that black women being close-minded is the reason for the current state of affairs is grossly simplifying the complex politics of attraction."*

Black Women Are Not to Blame for Low Marriage Rates

Latoya Peterson

Latoya Peterson is the editor of the blog Racialicious *and a writer whose work has been published in* Spin, Vibe, American Prospect, *and many other outlets. In the following viewpoint, she argues that it is wrong to blame low black marriage rates on black women refusing to date across racial lines. She argues that many black women, and many women in general, are not interested in marriage. For those who are, she says that prejudice against dating black women is often the factor that limits interracial dating. Finally, she argues that dating and relationships are very individual, and experts fail to capture this individuality when they focus on aggregate trends.*

As you read, consider the following questions:

1. Why does Peterson say black women wanted marriage during slavery?

2. What did the online dating site OkCupid find when it broke down response rates by race, according to the viewpoint?

3. What examples does Peterson give to show that finding the right person for a relationship is individual and often random?

Ralph Richard Banks, a Stanford professor, is the latest to attempt to cash in on the "single black woman" fearmongering that has been so popular in the media for the last two years—one that has led to countless articles, comedian-fronted *Nightline* panels, and a hilarious round of "let's blame the black church." Most recently, he's in the *Economist* peddling the same song black women have been hearing for years—a combination of "stop being so picky, date interracially, stop dating out of their class level (which is a reversal from older advice that black women should be open to dating blue-collar men), and marriage is the solution to most problems".

Listen to Black Women

The *Economist* article even provides a frightening chart on falling black marriage rates. But it doesn't provide an accurate picture of the dating environment. First of all, black women are hardly the only women currently re-evaluating marriage. The *Atlantic* has spent the last year documenting the changes in attitudes about rings and other shiny things. Historically speaking, marriage has been defined to mean what people need it to mean—from a way to secure economic security and partnership to a public declaration of love. In times of slavery, black women did want to be married—but the main focus was on creating a stable family unit, official or otherwise. More contemporary battles over marriage revolve around the changing needs of citizens, particularly those in same-sex relationships, or those with nontraditional families. And who said marriage is still the ultimate end goal? As Samhita Mukhopadhyay, author of *Outdated: Why Dating Is Ruining Your Love Life*, told me: "All of this conjecture about the failure rates of marriage is based on the assumption that all black women want to get married. There is so much talk about how it is impacting their lives but no one puts anything into studying what they actually want/need/feel." Not surprisingly, black women are lectured to about their love lives, not engaged in conversation.

There Is Prejudice in Dating

If we accept the premise that black women aren't doing well in the general dating market, there are other well-documented reasons for some of these gaps. Dating isn't exactly a bastion of political correctness. Back in 2007, Wendi Muse documented the environment over at Craigslist, noting that stereotypes were in full effect:

> In the world of online dating, where a user name, masked email address, and optional photo sharing means freedom to speak one's mind in complete anonymity, users frequently abandon political correctness and resort to exotification, stereotypes, and blatant racism when referring to racial/ethnic "others" in their attempts to choose a mate

Popular dating site OkCupid routinely crunches data about their users, looking at everything from the biggest lies in online dating to the best questions for a first date. One has to take their findings with a pinch of salt, but back in 2010 they made a stir by breaking down the information on response rates by race. The response was familiar to any black person who has attempted online dating:

> Men don't write black women back. Or rather, they write them back far less often than they should. Black women reply the most, yet get by far the fewest replies. Essentially every race—including other blacks—singles them out for the cold shoulder.

To be fair, black men also had a similarly low response rate. But to imply that black women being closed-minded is the reason for the current state of affairs is grossly simplifying the complex politics of attraction, particularly in societies that value some types of beauty more highly than others.

Generalizations Overlook Individual Circumstances

This leads me to my final pet peeve regarding so-called relationship experts. In their quest to sell books and make media appearances, they bulldoze the individual nature of the mating game in the rush to diagnose millions of people with the same problem. The truth is there are many reasons why people find themselves single. Sometimes, it's their own attitudes. But many other times, the timing just isn't right, their careers are too demanding, or they need to focus elsewhere. As a black woman who has been in a committed relationship for five years, nothing is more obvious to me than how random circumstance plays a major role in many happy relationships. If I hadn't missed a concert, I wouldn't know my boyfriend; if one of my friends hadn't gone to Mali with the Peace Corps, she would have never been on the same continent as her now-husband; if another friend hadn't missed her original train and hadn't been wearing a sweatshirt from her alma mater, she would have never met the man she would marry.

Dating, love, and marriage are far more complicated than self-proclaimed experts would have us believe. Statistics can show all kinds of trends, but ultimately, life, liberty, and the pursuit of happiness (in a relationship) is the province of each individual.

> "*I think the day will come when the lesbian and gay community will have its own* Loving v. Virginia,' *says David Buckel, the Marriage Project director for Lambda Legal.*"

The Loving Decision

Anna Quindlen

Anna Quindlen is the author of five best-selling novels, including Rise and Shine *and* Blessings, *and numerous nonfiction works. Until May 2009, she wrote the column "The Last Word" for* Newsweek. *In the following viewpoint, Quindlen argues that the struggle by gays and lesbians for same-sex marriage is similar to the civil rights struggle for interracial marriage as realized in the Supreme Court decision in* Loving v. Virginia *in 1967. Quindlen describes the opposition to same-sex marriage as bigotry, with the opponents unfairly appropriating God's name in support of their cause. Quindlen argues that Mildred Loving, the black woman who was the center of the* Loving *decision, believes that all Americans, regardless of race, sex, or sexual orientation, should have the same freedom, and that's what her struggle was about.*

As you read, consider the following questions:

1. What are the unmarried names of the husband and wife in the *Loving* decision? Where did they live and where were they married?

2. During the 2008 election, what state passed a proposition that reversed a court decision to allow same-sex marriage?

3. What two arguments of opponents of same-sex marriage does the author argue will have little effect in actual practice?

Same-sex marriage was beaten back at the ballot box. Now here's a history lesson on why victory is inevitable in the long run.

One of my favorite Supreme Court cases is *Loving v. Virginia*, and not just because it has a name that would delight any novelist. It's because it reminds me, when I'm downhearted, of the truth of the sentiment at the end of "Angels in America," Tony Kushner's brilliant play: "The world only spins forward."

Here are the facts of the case, and if they leave you breathless with disbelief and rage it only proves Kushner's point, and mine: Mildred Jeter and Richard Loving got married in Washington, D.C. They went home to Virginia, there to be rousted out of their bed one night by police and charged with a felony. The felony was that Mildred was black and Richard was white and they were therefore guilty of miscegenation, which is a $10 word for bigotry. Virginia, like a number of other states, considered cross-racial matrimony a crime at the time.

It turned out that it wasn't just the state that hated the idea of black people marrying white people. God was onboard, too, according to the trial judge, who wrote, "The fact that He separated the races shows that he did not intend for the races to mix." But the Supreme Court, which eventually heard the case, passed over the Almighty for the Constitution, which luckily has an equal-protection clause. "Marriage is one of the basic civil rights of man," the unanimous opinion striking down the couple's conviction said, "fundamental to our very existence and survival."

That was in 1967.

Fast-forward to Election Day 2008, and a flurry of state ballot propositions to outlaw gay marriage, all of which were successful. This is the latest wedge issue of the good-old-days crowd, supplanting abortion and immigration. They really put their backs into it this time around, galvanized by court decisions in three states ruling that it is discriminatory not to extend the right to marry to gay men and lesbians.

The most high-profile of those rulings, and the most high-profile ballot proposal, came in California. A state court gave its imprimatur to same-sex marriage in June; the electorate reversed that decision on Nov. 4 with the passage of Proposition 8, which defines marriage as only between a man and a woman. The opponents of gay marriage will tell you that the people have spoken. It's truer to say that money talks. The Mormons donated millions to the anti effort; the Knights of Columbus did, too. Like the judge who ruled in the *Loving* case, they said they were doing God's bidding. When I was a small child I always used to picture God on a cloud, with a beard. Now I picture God saying, "Why does all the worst stuff get done in my name?"

Just informationally, this is how things are going to go from here on in: two steps forward, one step back. Courts will continue to rule in some jurisdictions that there is no good reason to forbid same-sex couples from marrying. Legislatures in two states, New York and New Jersey, could pass a measure guaranteeing the right to matrimony to all, and both states have governors who have said they would sign such legislation.

Opponents will scream that the issue should be put to the people, as it was in Arizona, Florida and California. (Arkansas had a different sort of measure, forbidding unmarried couples from adopting or serving as foster parents. This will undoubtedly have the effect of leaving more kids without stable homes. For shame.) Of course if the issue in *Loving* had been put to the people, there is no doubt that many would have been delighted to make racial intermarriage a crime. That's why God invented courts.

The world only spins forward.

"I think the day will come when the lesbian and gay community will have its own *Loving v. Virginia*," says David Buckel, the Marriage Project director for Lambda Legal.

Yes, and then the past will seem as preposterous and mean-spirited as the events leading up to the *Loving* decision do today. After all, this is about one of the most powerful forces for good on earth, the determination of two human beings to tether their lives forever. The pitch of the opposition this year spoke to how far we have already come—the states in which civil unions and domestic partnerships are recognized, the families in which gay partners are welcome and beloved.

The antis argued that churches could be forced to perform same-sex unions, when any divorced Roman Catholic can tell you that the clergy refuse to officiate whenever they see fit. They argued that the purpose of same-sex marriage was the indoctrination of children, a popular talking point that has no basis in reality. As Ellen DeGeneres, who was married several months ago to the lovely Portia de Rossi (great dress, girl), said about being shaped by the orientation of those around you, "I was raised by two heterosexuals. I was surrounded by heterosexuals. Just everywhere I looked: heterosexuals. They did not influence me." As for the notion that allowing gay men and lesbians to marry will destroy conventional marriage, I have found heterosexuals perfectly willing to do that themselves.

The last word here goes to an authority on battling connubial bigotry. On the anniversary of the *Loving* decision last year, the bride wore tolerance. Mildred Loving, mother and grandmother, who once had cops burst into her bedroom because she was sleeping with her own husband, was quoted in a rare public statement saying she believed all Americans, "no matter their race, no matter their sex, no matter their sexual orientation, should have that same freedom to marry." She concluded, "That's what *Loving*, and loving, are all about."

> *"There is no use gay rights activists pretending they are being discriminated against in the same way that blacks or Jews were in the past, because they simply are not."*

Comparisons Between Opposition to Gay Marriage and Opposition to Interracial Marriage Are Ignorant and False

Brendan O'Neill

Brendan O'Neill is editor of the online magazine Spiked *and a columnist for the* Big Issue *and the* Australian. *In the following viewpoint, he argues that gay marriage is not comparable to interracial marriage because proponents of interracial marriage were campaigning for democratic inclusion in an already existing institution. Gay marriage proponents, he argues, are asking for the creation of a new institution. He says that two men marrying fundamentally changes the institution of marriage, which is built around a man and a woman. O'Neill says he does not necessarily oppose gay marriage but thinks that gay marriage activists should stop comparing their campaign to the campaign for interracial marriage. Instead, he argues, activists should explain why creating a new institution of marriage is needed and how it would benefit society.*

As you read, consider the following questions:

1. Why does O'Neill conclude that activists believe comparing gay marriage to interracial marriage is an argument winner?
2. How does O'Neill define the social institution of marriage?
3. What does O'Neill say the Supreme Court was right to argue in 1967?

As the debate about gay marriage heats up, the pro lobby is playing its trump card: It is arguing that opposing gay marriage today is as batty and backward as opposing interracial marriage was in the past. Activists clearly think this is an argument winner because they're repeating it ad nauseam. One writer says "same-sex marriage opponents don't realise how closely their rhetoric mirrors that of the anti-miscegenation activist". In California, gay rights activists continually cite the Supreme Court's stinging attack in 1967 on bans on interracial marriages, and call on the court to do "the right thing" once again by lifting the ban on gay marriage. An image doing the rounds on Twitter and Facebook shows modern-day campaigners against gay marriage alongside racists campaigning against interracial marriage in 1950s America, as if they were one and the same.

Old and New Social Institutions

Yet far from being an argument winner, this comparison between restrictions on interracial marriage and restrictions on gay marriage is utterly moronic; it is historically illiterate and politically opportunistic. Gay marriage supporters might like to fantasise that they are bravely struggling against an injustice as terrible as America's old bans on interracial marriage or European states' one-time bans on Jewish-Gentile marriages, but there is one very important difference between those who campaigned against bans on interracial marriage and those who campaign against restrictions on gay marriage: the anti-racist activists of old were calling for democratic equity within an already existing institution, whereas today's pro-gay marriage activists are calling for the creation of an entirely *new* institution.

The reason bans on interracial marriage were an abomination, something worth campaigning tooth and catapult against, is because they denied people equity within an important social institution—the state-recognised and approved bond between a man and a woman, usually, though not always, for the purposes of procreation. This institution has profound historical, social and cultural roots, and in denying equal access to it to certain men and women, simply on the basis of their skin colour or their religious beliefs, old societies were behaving in an extremely illiberal and undemocratic fashion. So the Supreme Court was quite right when it argued in 1967 that bans on interracial marriage were a violation of individuals' "vital personal rights, [which are] essential to the orderly pursuit of happiness by free men". If society says it is good for men and women to marry, yet then denies certain men and women the right to marry, it is committing an act of prejudicial repression.

Gay Marriage Is Different

Gay marriage is very different, because such an institution, the state-approved union of two men, has never existed before. Where black and white lovers or Jewish/Gentile sweethearts once demanded, rightly and bravely, equity within an existing social institution, gay rights activists today are actually demanding the creation of a brand new, historically unprecedented institution—one in which two men can, in the eyes of the state and society, form a marital union. There is no use gay rights activists pretending they are being discriminated against in the same way that blacks or Jews were in the past, because they simply are not; indeed, it is a bit off to compare the modern gay desire to fashion a completely new institution with the once brutal exclusion of certain groups of people from an *existing* and very long-standing institution simply because they fell in love with people of a different pigmentation or religious persuasion.

Perhaps gay marriage should be introduced: who knows? I'm undecided (though not for religious reasons—I'm an atheist), as are many religious people and ordinary members of the public. Yet clearly there are many homosexuals who want such an institution to be created, and they could be right; certainly society ought to have some system through which gay couples can publicly commit to one another. But let's at least be honest about what is happening here: People are campaigning for the setting up of a special and new institution. If you want to do that, then go for it, and try to win people over to your belief that this new institution is necessary and good. But please stop flattering your activism by comparing yourselves to those brave souls who took a stand against the stark denial of equity and democratic rights brought about by bans on interracial marriage in the past.

Periodical and Internet Sources Bibliography

The following articles have been selected to supplement the diverse views presented in this chapter.

W.T. Beals	"Strict Parents Against Interracial Marriage," *I Am Asian* (blog), Experience Project, December 14, 2009. www.experienceproject.com/stories /Am-Asian/.
Ta-Nehisi Coates	"Race and Gay Marriage in Perspective," *Atlantic*, August 3, 2010.
David Morse	"Interracial Marriage Is Widely Accepted, but Not for Ad Families," *The Big Tent* (blog), *Ad Age*, March 16, 2012. http://adage.com/article/ the-big-tent.
Erin Gloria Ryan	"Can White Men Fix Black Women's Relationships?," *Jezebel* (blog), August 7, 2011. http:// jezebel.com.
Susan Saulny	"Interracial Marriage Seen Gaining Wide Acceptance," *New York Times*, February 16, 2012.
Kate Sheppard	"'The Loving Story': How an Interracial Couple Changed a Nation," *Mother Jones*, February 13, 2012.
Alan Shlemon	"Is Banning Same-Sex Marriage Like Banning Interracial Marriage?," *STR Place Blog*, May 16, 2012. http://strplace.wordpress.com.
Rachel L. Swarns	"For Asian-American Couples, a Tie That Binds," *New York Times*, March 30, 2012.
Margaret Talbot	"Wedding Bells," *New Yorker*, May 21, 2012.
Dawn Turner Trice	"Interracial Marriage Is Not Just a Black and White Issue," *Chicago Tribune*, February 20, 2012.

CHAPTER 4

What Issues Confront Children in Multiracial Families?

Chapter Preface

Members of multiracial families can face discrimination—both subtle and overt—as well as other difficulties. John Chatz, in a June 25, 2012, article for *Chicago Now*, wrote about some of his family's experiences: Chatz is white; his wife is black, and their daughter is light-skinned. He related one particularly telling incident:

> A couple approached my wife in the Starbucks parking lot and the woman asked, "We've seen you in here a few times recently, do the baby's parents live in the neighborhood?"
>
> "I'm the mom." Women can be cold and much scarier than men when crossed, especially when it involves family. It doesn't take a lot of words to make a point.
>
> "Oh my God, I'm so sorry, I just thought . . ."
>
> "Mmmmm hmmmm."

Chatz's anecdotes mostly, like this one, involve relatively minor incidents. The prejudice that black parents of white children experience can, by contrast, be quite painful. A black writer of a January 12, 2011, post at the Experience Project, for example, related the teasing and cruelty her light-skinned daughter faced. The writer says that classmates cornered her daughter, Kayla, at school and demanded, "'What the heck are you?' You are not black, you are not white, you are not Hispanic what are you. She came home crying."

Black parents who adopt white children can also face social pressure and misunderstanding. In the United States, there are a disproportionate number of black children in the adoption system, and white people are sometimes less willing to adopt black babies. There is, therefore, considerable pressure for black families to adopt black children.

Still, in some cases, white children do end up with black families. Ashley Hopkinson, in an October 24, 2011, essay at the Grio, reports on one such family. Mary Riley, a black woman who took in three white brothers for foster care, eventually fell in love with them and decided to adopt them. As Riley said, "I couldn't let them go, and I was afraid they were going to get separated from each other." Riley added, "Sometimes people stare at us and ask questions.... But, I accept these boys and they accept us, so I ain't worried about anybody else."

Tony Dokoupil, in an April 22, 2009, article at the Daily Beast, writes about another black family with an adopted white child. Mark and Terri Riding, who have two children of their own, adopted Katie O'Dea-Smith after Terri came to know the child through her job as a social worker. Dokoupil chronicles a day with the Ridings during which people are constantly and visibly unable to accept that Katie is their child. Dokoupil says the Ridings attribute this disbelief to racism, and he says, "it's hard to blame them. To shadow them for a day ... to feel the unease, notice the negative attention and realize that the same note of fear isn't in the air when they attend [to] their two biological children." Mark Riding adds, "I've never felt more self-consciously black than while holding our little white girl's hand in public."

Black families with white children may have to overcome unique prejudices, but other multiracial families also face challenges. The following viewpoints discuss some of the issues and controversies surrounding multiracial families and their children.

| "*Researchers are finding that multiracial kids can sometimes be better socially adjusted than single-race offspring.*"

La. Interracial Marriage: Is Life Tougher for Biracial Kids?

Patrik Jonsson

Patrik Jonsson is a staff writer for the Christian Science Monitor. *In the following viewpoint, he reports that biracial children were once thought to face psychological and social barriers and were even thought to be physically inferior. However, Jonsson says, today there is much more acceptance of biracial marriages and children, and some studies even show biracial children having some physical and psychological advantages. Certainly, Jonsson concludes, children's well-being is no longer seen as an adequate reason to prevent biracial marriages.*

As you read, consider the following questions:

1. Who is Keith Bardwell, and why have his actions been controversial, according to Jonsson?

2. What physical advantage have researchers found that biracial children have, according to the viewpoint?

3. As a biracial woman, what is the one thing Phoebe Hinton says people won't accept her doing?

Louisiana justice of the peace Keith Bardwell refused to marry a white woman and a black man reportedly because he believed that children of an interracial marriage would suffer socially.

That view was once common in the United States, and might have had some basis decades ago when such marriages were taboo and multiracial families were sometimes ostracized. But today, not only are mixed-race children widely accepted but some research suggests they might even have some social advantages.

Researchers are finding that multiracial kids can sometimes be better socially adjusted than single-race offspring. And with the high-profile success of multiracial progeny such as Tiger Woods, Halle Berry, and President Obama (who at his first press conference as president described himself as a "mutt"), stereotypes about the split world of the "tragic mulatto" have long fallen by the wayside.

The American Civil Liberties Union is now threatening a lawsuit if Mr. Bardwell, veteran justice of the peace at Tangipahoa Parish, doesn't step down. The group calls Bardwell's refusal to issue a marriage license to Beth Humphrey (who is white) and Terence McKay (who is black) both "tragic and illegal."

"I'm not a racist," Bardwell told a local newspaper. "I do ceremonies for black couples right here in my house. My main concern is for the children."

The "Tragic Mulatto"

Refusing to issue marriage licenses for reasons of race has been illegal in the US since the Supreme Court in 1967 struck down anti-miscegenation laws in 16 states, mostly in the South.

Research on mixed-race children once focused on the social and psychological problems that can arise from not feeling like a full member of any racial group. That notion permeated early 20th-century American literature through the figure of the "tragic mulatto," who did not fit in with either the black or white world.

As recently as 1968, the psychologist J.D. Teicher wrote, "Although the burden of the Negro child is recognized as a heavy one, that of the Negro-White child is seen to be even heavier."

The idea that mixed-race children were biologically inferior to white or black kids was also widespread in the South, and often formed the basis of anti-miscegenation laws during Jim Crow years. (Researchers have found that not only is that not true, but that mixed-race offspring tend to be overall more physically attractive than their peers.)

Changing Views

But loosening of marriage laws and more-accepting social mores have transformed perceptions of multiracial families. For one thing, there are now 7 million mixed-race kids in the US, up from 500,000 in the 1970s.

A 2008 study of 182 mixed-race high school kids in California found that these kids didn't focus on exclusionary features like skin color or hair texture when thinking about themselves, but instead, they appeared to feel that their heritage made them "unique."

The kids are able to "place one foot in the majority and one in the minority group, and in this way might be buffered against the negative consequences of feeling tokenized," the study authors wrote in the *Journal of Social Issues*. The students surveyed included those with mixed Asian, Hispanic heritage.

Other studies suggest that while mixed-race kids may no longer feel the burden of discrimination, they still face unique challenges. A 2008 study led by Harvard researchers found that mixed-race adolescents tend to engage in risky behavior outside of school at higher rates than average and also fare "somewhat worse on measures of psychological well-being."

The reality for many mixed-race children probably lies somewhere between liberating and restrictive. On a Yale University blog this year, biracial student Phoebe Hinton wrote: "I am lucky enough to have an excuse flowing in my veins to do whatever . . . I want: there are some things white people do and . . . I'll do them. There are some things black people do, and . . . I'll do them."

"Pretty much the only thing people won't accept me doing," she adds, "is continuing to identify as neither black nor white, but an amalgam of the two."

Whether biracial children in rural Louisiana experience the same confidence in their identity—in a region where race arguably still hangs heavier than other parts of the country—is an open question.

Even if they don't, Bardwell, the justice of the peace, will be hard-pressed to convince anybody—including potentially the US Justice Department—that that's any of his business.

| "Multiracial individuals who possess a true multiracial identity are raised in an environment incorporating the values and beliefs of both racial groups."

Multiracial Students: What School Counselors Need to Know

Henry L. Harris

Henry L. Harris is an associate professor in the Department of Counseling, College of Education, University of North Carolina–Charlotte. In the following viewpoint, Harris outlines some stereotypes that people think of when they interact with multiracial students and offers advice to school counselors to help overcome these stereotypes. Stereotypical assumptions may include, for example, the idea that multiracial children are confused about their racial identity or that they identify with the parent of color. School counselors should try to recognize when they use stereotypes of multiracial students, confront their own feelings, and resolve them. In addition, school counselors should try to develop an environment in their school that embraces cultural diversity.

Henry L. Harris, "Multiracial Students: What School Counselors Need to Know," ERIC Digest, September 2003.

As you read, consider the following questions:

1. How many people in the 2000 US Census indicated that they belonged to more than one race, according to the author?

2. Should people assume that a multiracial individual will feel more welcome in the minority community, according to the author?

3. In what three ways do parents tend to foster racial identity development in their multiracial children, according to the author?

Multiracial individuals represent an expanding population of America's diverse society. Results from Census 2000 showed that of the total 281.4 million people in the United States, 6.8 million or 2.4% of the population indicated their background consisted of more than just one race. Ninety-three percent of the multiracial population reported belonging to two racial groups, 6% reported belonging to three racial groups and the remaining 1% reported belonging to more than four races. Nearly 3 million, or 42% of respondents within the two or more races population were under the age of 18 (U.S. Bureau of Census, 2001), and it is safe to assume that many are students in our public school systems.

This digest provides school counselors with basic information necessary to gain a better understanding of students from multiracial backgrounds. It also will address stereotypes commonly associated with multiracial students, their unique needs, and how school counselors can better respond to this growing population.

Stereotypes and Myths Regarding Multiracial Individuals

Historically, multiracial individuals have been stereotyped as socially inept individuals who lack culture and are destined to have social and psychological problems associated with racial identity (Stonequist, 1937), thus leading a confused life because they will never fit in or gain acceptance to any racial group (Nakashima, 1992). Too often we hear clichés such as, "I have nothing against interracial marriages, I just feel sorry for the children because they will not be accepted or know who to identify with."

According to Brown (1990), to automatically suggest that multiracial individuals will likely have identity problems as a result of their background typically refers to the view that these individuals do not fit neatly into socially defined racial categories and as a result they have trouble determining their position, role, and status in society. It is important for school counselors to treat multiracial students as individuals first and avoid making false assumptions about them based upon characteristics associated with multiracial group membership.

Another stereotype associated with multiracial individuals is the belief that they are more accepted in the minority community and should therefore identify with the parent of color (Kerwin & Ponterotto, 1995). This perspective is associated with elements of the "one drop rule," which originated from the belief that each race had its own specific blood type and just one drop of "Negro blood" provided enough evidence to classify that person as black, regardless of their physical appearance (Valentine, 1995). The ultimate goal behind the "one drop rule" was to promote segregation and discourage social interaction between blacks and whites. However, when multiracial individuals do not culturally identify with both parents, Sebring (1985) contends this may cause them to experience feelings of disloyalty and enormous guilt over their rejection of one parent for the other. Therefore it is crucial for multiracial children to assume a multiracial identity.

Finally, some believe that multiracial individuals do not like to discuss their racial heritage. On the contrary, Kerwin and Ponterotto (1995) indicated that when multiracial individuals are approached in a genuine and caring manner, they do not mind such inquiries and may associate this interest with acceptance and support.

How School Counselors Should Respond

School counselors should first develop an awareness of their own personal feelings toward multiracial individuals and multiracial families (Nishimura, 1995; Wardle, 1992). If erroneous or preconceived notions exist about multiracial children or multiracial families, they must be confronted and emotionally resolved if school counselors are to maximize their effectiveness. School counselors should also strive to educate themselves about the emotional needs of multiracial children by reading literature, attending workshops, and talking with multiracial families.

The American Academy of Child and Adolescent Psychiatry (AACAP, 1999) reports that research focusing on multiracial individuals has shown that: 1) multiracial children have similar self-esteem levels and experience psychiatric problems at no greater rate when compared to other children; 2) the racial identity of children from the same multiracial family can vary because identity is influenced by factors including family attachments, family support, experiences with diverse racial and ethnic groups, and individual physical features; 3) multiracial children may develop a public identity with the minority race yet also hold a private multiracial identity with family and friends as a way to cope with societal prejudice; 4) multiracial children may encounter obstacles that make it more difficult for them to accept and value the culture of both parents when parents divorce; and 5) multiracial individuals who possess a true multiracial identity are raised in an environment incorporating the values and beliefs of both racial groups and are generally happier than multiracial individuals who identify with the race of only one parent (AACAP, 1999).

Multiracial individuals, because of their unique developmental history, will typically possess more insight and sensitivity to both racial groups than single race children because they have the opportunity to personally experience what the racial identity of each implies.

Racial Identity Development for Multiracial Individuals

School counselors should become knowledgeable about the different developmental aspects of racial identity for multiracial individuals. Models developed by Poston (1990) and Kerwin and Ponterotto (1995) are helpful resources to school counselors as they learn about this population of students. Learning how to promote the racial identity development of multiracial children is also a common issue for parents. Parents tend to:

1. deny or minimize the significance of race as an important factor in identity development,

2. incorporate the identity of only one parent by immersing the family solely in that parent's particular community, or

3. encourage multiracial children to embrace all aspects of their multiracial heritage.

McRoy and Zurcher (1983) identified a number of significant factors that help facilitate the positive development of racial identity of multiracial children:

- Multiracial children should be encouraged to acknowledge and discuss their racial heritage with their parents, extended family members, and other important individuals in their lives.

- Parents must be able to perceive their child's racial heritage as being different from their own. They should be willing to make changes that will contribute to the development of a positive racial identity in the child.

- Multiracial children should be given the opportunity to develop relationships with people from culturally diverse backgrounds. This can be accomplished by attending a culturally diverse school and by living in a culturally diverse neighborhood.

- The family should form an identity as a multiracial unit.

These factors are significant because even though societal attitudes towards multiracial families and multiracial individuals have improved, stereotypes and prejudice are still likely to be confronted. Harris (2002) found that school counselors validated this perspective. They strongly believed that schools are a microcosm of a society that does not genuinely accept multiracial children, thus the question follows: how genuinely are multiracial children accepted in schools?

The multiracial population in the school setting will continue to increase as our nation's population becomes more diverse. Therefore it is important for school counselors to have an accurate understanding of multiracial individuals and their families. School counselors should work to create a cultural environment in their school setting that embraces diversity because, as Harris (2002) found:

- School counselors who were employed in schools that actively promoted cultural diversity and awareness programs held more accurate perceptions of multiracial children.

- School counselors who were in schools that did not actively promote cultural diversity and awareness programs were more likely to inaccurately: 1) believe that racial identity issues were the major cause of emotional problems for multiracial children, 2) support the perception that multiracial children should identify primarily with the minority parent, and 3) categorize multiracial children with the minority parent.

- School counselors in school settings that actively promoted cultural diversity and awareness programs believed living in a racially diverse neighborhood was helpful in facilitating positive development of racial identity for multiracial children.

Conclusion

This digest has introduced some of the issues that multiracial students face. The school counselor can help to create a positive environment for these students by promoting cultural diversity and awareness programs that debunk myths associated with multiracial individuals. Further, school counselors should be aware of differences between multiracial students and treat them as individuals first. Finally, school counselors should recognize the unique heritage of multiracial individuals and some of the problems they may encounter as a result of their heritage. Multiracial individuals need to feel genuinely valued, supported, and understood and school counselors can play an influential role in helping to communicate this message.

References

American Academy of Child and Adolescent Psychiatry (1999). Facts for families: Multiracial children. No. 71, www.aacap.org/publications/factsfam/71.htm.

Brown, P. M. (1990). Biracial identity and social marginality. Child and Adolescent Social Work, 7, 319–337.

Harris, H. L. (2002). School counselors' perceptions of biracial children: A pilot study. Professional School Counseling, 6, 120–129.

Kerwin, K., & Ponterotto, J. G. (1995). Biracial identity development. In J. G. Ponterotto, J. M. Casas, L. A. Suzuki, & C. M. Alexander (Eds.), Handbook of multicultural counseling (pp. 199–217). Thousands Oaks, CA: Sage.

McRoy, R. G., & Zurcher, L. A. (1983). Transracial and in-racial adoptees: The adolescent years. Springfield, IL: Charles C. Thomas.

Nakashima, C. L. (1992). An invisible monster: The creation and denial of racially mixed people in America. In Maria P. P. Root (Ed.), Racially mixed people in America (pp. 162–180). Newbury Park, CA: Sage.

Nishimura, N. (1995). Addressing the needs of biracial children: An issue for school counselors in a multicultural school environment. The School Counselor, 43, 52–57.

Poston, W. S. C. (1990). The biracial identity development model: A needed addition. Journal of Counseling and Development, 69,152–155.

Sebring, D. L. (1985). Considerations in counseling interracial children. Journal of Non-White Concerns, 13, 3–9.

Stonequist, E. V. (1937). The marginal man: A study in personality and culture and conflict. New York: Russell & Russell.

U.S. Bureau of Census. (2001). Mapping census 2000: The geography of U.S. diversity. Washington, DC: U.S. Government Printing Office.

Valentine, G. (1995). Shades of gray: The conundrum of color categories. Teaching Tolerance, 49, 47.

Wardle, F. (1992). Supporting biracial children in the school setting. Education and Treatment of Children, 15, 63–172.

> *"We take in kids that would've had a bad family life, and we can see to it that they don't, and that they have a happy family. Family is everything."*

"Family Is Everything"

Melanie Stetson Freeman

Melanie Stetson Freeman is a staff writer for the Christian Science Monitor. *In the following viewpoint, Stetson Freeman describes the joys that one family has found in adopting twelve children, many of them of a different race from the adoptive parents and from the other adopted children. Many of the children have disabilities, but the dire predictions about potential problems did not deter the family parents. The parents focused on the importance of the family in each child's life, considered each child their own, and fell in love with each child. Taking care of all the children involves home schooling, getting help from the community, and giving the children themselves chores to do, which often involves taking care of a brother or sister. State and community workers applaud the work that the family has done and testify to how the family and community have been enriched by these adoptions.*

As you read, consider the following questions:

1. What races do the adoptive children come from in the family discussed in the viewpoint?

2. For how long a period might a foster parent look after a foster child, according to the viewpoint?

3. Why is it easier for the mother to home school her children than to send them to public school, according to the viewpoint?

*B*irmingham, Ala.—An Alabama couple adopted 12 children, nine of whom have special needs.

Beverly and Sam Gardner never thought they'd have 16 kids. But after their four biological children were born, they started adopting—and couldn't stop. Eventually, 12 more children were added to the family. Each one has a story.

"Chip [now 10] was 6 months old when we got him. He'd been put in a book bag, zipped up, and put in the trash," Bev says, explaining the early days of one of her children. He was rescued after the house where he lived caught fire and one of the firemen discovered him in the garbage behind the house.

"Johnny [now 12] was 3-1/2 months early because of his mother's drug abuse. She basically abandoned him in the hospital," Bev continues.

The Gardners adopted Johnny, who can't see and had been diagnosed with cerebral palsy, despite warnings from doctors that he might be a "vegetable."

"He definitely is not!" his mother says.

The Gardners' adopted children are black, white, Latina, and biracial. Nine of them have special needs. None of that bothered the Gardners. Neither did predicted problems.

"Once you fall in love with a child, that's your child, and all the fear just goes away," Bev says. "Once we heard the terrible stories, we couldn't say no."

Bev and Sam both come from big families. After three of their biological children arrived prematurely, the couple decided that since they wanted more, they would adopt. They are Caucasian, but were happy to adopt black or biracial children, who are harder to place.

After the Gardners' first two adoptions, they came into contact with state organizations that help find homes for at-risk children. After hearing the stories about these children, the Gardners became foster parents, caring for more than a hundred special-needs children for periods as short as a couple hours to as long as a few years.

Whenever parents gave up the rights to any of these children over the years, the Gardners adopted them. "More than likely, if they left [the Gardners'], they would've gone to a group home or some kind of place for special-needs children," Sam says. He and his wife felt it was important to give them a real home.

Older children and children with disabilities are very difficult to place, says James Tucker, a lawyer and associate director of the Alabama Disabilities Advocacy Program. Combine the two, and it's almost impossible to find families willing to take on the challenge.

"Children that come to [the Gardner] home do not get turned out," he adds. "We see an alarming number of cases where kids come into foster homes and are not part of that home. With [the Gardners], there's never a doubt that those children are, and remain, a part of that family."

The work involved in having so large a family is constant. "I've had people come in and say: 'You need nurses,'" Bev says, "but my children aren't sick. They have disabilities, but they're healthy, they're whole."

Everyone Pitches In

The Gardners' six-bedroom, two-story home is surprisingly calm and amazingly clean. All 13 children living at home, ranging in age from 6 to 28, have chores.

Brian, who is 9, has become little Lynden's constant companion. Since she can't walk, he pushes her around in her stroller and entertains her with rub-on tattoos.

Tony, 16, helps care for Johnny, 12, and Destin, 14, changing their diapers and helping to feed them. Tony carries Johnny wherever he needs to go—even though they're almost the same size.

Bev home-schools eight of the children. "They weren't getting what they needed and were getting left behind," she explains. "I know what my kids need. I know how slow they go. We can make things the way they can do the best, and they've done well."

She had doubts about home-schooling in the beginning. "I never thought I could do it. But it's actually been easier. Sending them to public school was harder. This is a good fit for us."

Support from Many Sources

Supporting such a large family is challenging—especially with healthcare costs and the special medical equipment some of the children require. Sam has worked as a shoe salesman at a local department store for 30 years.

The family receives subsidies from the state for the most severely challenged kids, and the community helps.

A local company has bought the children's Christmas presents since 2001. A church group renovated the family's kitchen and dining room.

"A lot of people [who help] say: 'We do this because we can't do what you're doing, so we want to give back in some way,'" Bev says.

"Having one [child] with a disability is a lot of work," says Rod White, director of a baseball league for special-needs children and adults—where the Gardner family has its own team.

"Having a family of children with disabilities is something I can't comprehend," he adds. "And look at [Bev]. She always has a smile on her face. Just the fact that she would take all these kids in, kids that nobody else wanted, and make them her own, to me just says it all."

"I've always pulled for the underdog," Sam says. "We take in kids that would've had a bad family life, and we can see to it that they don't, and that they have a happy family. Family is everything."

> *"Black adoptees tell a similar tale: They felt estranged from the people around them who they instinctively knew from an early age were different from them, and yet cut off from their own racial identity and culture."*

Transracial Adoptions Can Present Challenges for Adopted Children

Ron Claiborne and Hanna Siegel

Ron Claiborne is the weekend news anchor of the television news show Good Morning America; *Hanna Siegel is a reporter for ABC News. In the following viewpoint, they report that some black children adopted by white families feel disconnected from their culture and their black identity. The authors suggest that white families adopting black children should make an effort to move to integrated neighborhoods and connect their children to other black people and black communities. The authors conclude that white parents should be aware of the difficulties of raising black children.*

Ron Claiborne and Hanna Siegel, "Transracial Adoption Can Provide a Loving Family and an Identity Struggle," ABC News, March 3, 2010.

As you read, consider the following questions:

1. What does Phil Bertelsen mean when he refers to the "gratitude complex"?

2. According to the authors, why did transracial adoption in the United States end for almost twenty years?

3. Why do the Scoppas feel they do not need to apologize for adopting Haitian children?

They are images of joy, images of happy endings among so much tragedy.

A few days ago, Duke and Lisa Scoppa adopted two Haitian orphans, 4-year-old Erickson and 4-month-old Therline.

"I just always felt like it would be a really enriching experience for us and for everybody involved, really," Lisa Scoppa said.

Among the things that lie ahead for the Haitian children adopted by white American parents are a better life materially and a chance to grow up in a loving family.

Outside Looking In

But some black children who were adopted by white parents say there's another side of the story.

"I didn't feel like I was seen or understood," said Phil Bertelsen, who was 4 when he was adopted by a white family and then raised in a mostly white New Jersey suburb.

Bertelsen and other black adoptees tell a similar tale: They felt estranged from the people around them who they instinctively knew from an early age were different from them, and yet cut off from their own racial identity and culture.

"In my teens, I became hungry to be a part of some kind of black community, black identity," Bertelsen said. "What was missed primarily was, you know, strong familiar representations of black life other than the ones I was getting through popular culture and otherwise."

He grew up to be a documentary filmmaker and made his first movie, *Outside Looking In*, about transracial adoption. In it, he confronts his own parents for the first time.

"Ultimately, I am a part of your family," he told them in the film. "I use my name with pride. But I am also an African-American in your family and, you know, you have to see me as that."

In response, his mother said softly, "Maybe we were naive. Maybe we were. I don't know."

Bertelsen said in an interview that adoptees "don't tend to want to shake the tree too much. I call it the gratitude complex. We finally get this family, whomever they are, that we can call our own and so we adjust, we adapt, we learn to go along and get along and that's what I did."

"So in a way, home became a safe haven . . . but it was a total disconnect from the world outside and so you end up, I ended up, internalizing the questions," he said.

Through his movie, Bertelsen said, he was able to say what he had always wanted to say: "See me. This is who I am."

"It was a hard truth for my parents," he said.

"People don't like discomfort but when you're adopting a child from another race, another country, it's very important that families understand that they are going to put themselves outside of their comfort zone to really understand what their experience is going to be for the child. . . . Otherwise, the child is going to be neglected plain, and simple," Bertelsen said.

An Identity Struggle

For more than 20 years, starting in 1972, transracial adoptions in the United States all but ended after the National [Association of] Black Social Workers condemned them as cultural genocide.

White Parents and Racism

White parents do generally teach their adopted [black] children to be proud of their backgrounds and to have a positive sense of self-worth, but ... the white parents also communicate, consciously and unconsciously, a quite different lesson that privileges white framing, characteristics, norms, and ways of doing and being. In effect, their black children are taught that whiteness is normal and that they should mostly conform to the contours and requirements of that whiteness.

The authors [in the anthology *White Parents, Black Children: Experiencing Transracial Adoption*] make clear that they are not primarily blaming white parents for their parenting styles. Instead, these researchers have examined what it means to adopt and love a black child within a society fundamentally grounded in white-imposed racism. ... White adoptive parents are seriously handicapped by operating out of the dominant white racial frame, which they did not invent but which they regularly operate out of, and typically with little critical awareness of its significance or impact on them. As a result, most white parents are not only unprepared to raise black children, but often unconsciously or half-consciously racist in their everyday operations and actions in regard to their children, because they too operate out of the dominant racial frame.

*Joe R. Feagin, "Foreword,"
in Darron T. Smith, Cardell K. Jacobson, and
Brenda G. Juárez,* White Parents, Black Children:
Experiencing Transracial Adoption.
Lanham, MD: Rowman & Littlefield, 2011, p. viii.

The group takes a softer line now but it still maintains that it's better for children when parents are from the same racial or ethnic background.

"You're only a child once and for a minute," association president [Gloria] Batiste-Roberts said. "And children deserve the right to be with people who look like them, people who understand what they are going through, who understand their culture."

The Spence-Chapin Adoption agency in New York City, which facilitates many transracial adoptions, urged white parents who adopt black children to move to an integrated neighborhood, send their child to an integrated school and expose them to other black people.

"This is what I tell people," Rita Taddonio, who directs the agency's Adoption Resource Center, said. "If you look around your table and your guests are all the same color, if you don't have diversity around your kitchen table then you shouldn't be adopting a child of a different color."

There are ways to help your child cope, she said. "We recommend parents connect to the black community, that they make sure they have friends in those areas, that they go to a black church or be part of the community as well," she said. "Every parent's job is to help them form an identity, it's just an additional layer of complexity when your child's identity has pieces of it that you don't own."

Transracial Adoption in America

These days, many white families are rushing to adopt Haitian orphans after the earthquake [in January 2010] left so many children without parents or families.

The Scoppas said they will make every effort to connect Erickson and Therline to their Haitian and black roots. But they did not apologize for adopting black children.

"If there are no black families that want to adopt them and we want to adopt them, and make them part of our lives and give them as much love as possible, then I don't know why that's so wrong," Duke Scoppa said.

Not wrong, say some of those who grew up black in a white family . . . but not easy, either.

> "The destabilization of racial identity begins with a fact: Sexual relationships between blacks and whites, both romantic and coercive, have existed since the earliest days of slavery."

Exploring Grays in a Black-and-White World

Julia M. Klein

Julia M. Klein is a Philadelphia-based cultural reporter. In the following viewpoint, she discusses two books about the fluidity of racial identity in the United States. She argues that black and white people in America have always had relationships and children and that racial status has therefore always been fluid. The "one-drop rule," which states that any black ancestor or drop of "black blood" classifies an individual as black, was sometimes enforced, but more often, she says, people used a combination of ancestry and appearance to assign people to racial categories. As a result, Klein asserts light-skinned people with some black ancestry were often able to adopt identities as white people.

As you read, consider the following questions:

1. Who wrote *Slaves in the Family*, and what is the book about, according to Klein?

Julia M. Klein, "Exploring Grays in a Black-and-White World," *Pacific Standard*, July 9, 2011. Reproduced by permission.

2. According to Sharfstein, who were the Gibsons, and how did they change their racial identity?

3. What does Klein say happened when a white Clamorgan woman had a dark-skinned baby?

Two new books explore the intersection of race and identity in America by investigating families whose biracial members might—or might not—"pass" as white.

Defining racial identity in the United States has always been a fraught enterprise, involving shifting intersections of law, custom, class, ancestry and choice. Physical appearance and money have mattered, but so have family history and community attitudes—and not always in the ways we might suspect.

Two intriguing new books—Daniel J. Sharfstein's *The Invisible Line: Three American Families and the Secret Journey from Black to White* and Julie Winch's *The Clamorgans: One Family's History of Race in America*—underline the fluidity of racial categories over nearly three centuries of American history. And, thanks to legal records and other archival evidence, they offer illuminating detail about precisely how—and often why—individuals circumvented or manipulated these categories.

The destabilization of racial identity begins with a fact: Sexual relationships between blacks and whites, both romantic and coercive, have existed since the earliest days of slavery. Edward Ball's National Book Award–winning 1998 volume, *Slaves in the Family*, recounted his search for descendants of slaves owned by his family of South Carolina planters—and his discovery that some of them were his cousins. A decade later, Annette Gordon-Reed imaginatively reconstructed the lives of the mixed-race Hemings family and their ties to Thomas Jefferson in her 2009 Pulitzer Prize–winning *The Hemingses of Monticello: An American Family*.

As Jefferson did with the Hemings children, planters sometimes emancipated their slave progeny. After a generation or two, intermarriage between light-skinned blacks and whites produced children who could pass for white, and, in racist, segregated America, had strong economic and social motives for doing so. Three of the Hemingses now believed by historians to have been fathered by Jefferson with Sally Hemings assumed white identities; only Madison Hemings remained in the black community.

American popular culture has long embraced the "one-drop rule," stipulating that anyone with any African ancestry, discernible or not, was black. This view, for example, prompts a tragic plot twist in Edna Ferber's 1926 novel *Show Boat* and its Jerome Kern–Oscar Hammerstein musical adaptation. (Nor is the concept just a historical oddity: Actress Halle Berry recently cited the one-drop rule in a custody battle over her daughter.)

In practice, though, as Sharfstein notes, the legal demarcation between white and black has varied among states and over time. In most Southern states through the beginning of the 20th century, one black great-grandparent made someone legally black; other states, such as Virginia, required a black grandparent (though since the relevant ancestor could well have been the product of racial mixing, any standard remained murky and difficult to enforce).

But where racial divisions seemed murkiest, racial ideology could harden. In Louisiana, where "it was famously difficult to distinguish one race from the other at a glance," Sharfstein observes, whites believed all the more fiercely in racial supremacy. "The porous nature of the color line," he writes, "required eternal vigilance."

Sharfstein's achievement in *The Invisible Line* is to show, in meticulous detail, how three American families, representing different time periods, social strata and geographic communities, nevertheless made the transition from black to white. For the Gibsons, originally free people of color in colonial Virginia, a move to South Carolina and the acquisition of land erased their racial identity. By the time of the Civil War, they were white Southern aristocrats, proudly serving in the Confederate Army and opposing Reconstruction. Their African origins weren't even a memory—just a slur that family members publicly dismissed and privately fretted over.

Sharfstein, an associate professor at Vanderbilt Law School, argues that it could be advantageous not just for biracial families to define themselves as white, but for their communities as well. He illustrates this point with the Spencers. Though Jordan Spencer, the child of an interracial relationship, was dark-skinned, his tight-knit 19th-century Appalachian Kentucky community nevertheless preferred to integrate him as a neighbor by regarding him as white.

Finally, there were the Walls, whose white ancestor, Stephen Wall, was a North Carolina planter. He freed his three biracial offspring, sent them to Ohio to be educated, and willed them his considerable wealth. His descendants, most notably O.S.B. Wall, became abolitionists, Reconstruction leaders and civil rights activists. But despite a proud African-American legacy, later generations of light-skinned Walls, confronting segregation, began assuming white identities, even at the cost of downward mobility and social isolation.

At times, they also faced legal setbacks: In 1909, the District of Columbia courts rejected Isabel Wall's right to attend a whites-only school, despite her fair skin and considerable white ancestry. But George Spencer, Jordan Spencer's grandson, had better luck in the Virginia Supreme Court with a slander suit he brought against a former friend who had called his family "God damned Negros." The 1914 ruling in his favor (and others like it) helped make the South "safe" for Jim Crow, Sharfstein argues counterintuitively, because it shored up the security of established "white" families with question-

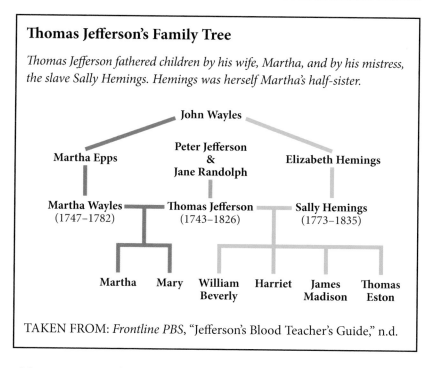

Thomas Jefferson's Family Tree

Thomas Jefferson fathered children by his wife, Martha, and by his mistress, the slave Sally Hemings. Hemings was herself Martha's half-sister.

John Wayles

Martha Epps   Peter Jefferson & Jane Randolph   Elizabeth Hemings

Martha Wayles (1747–1782)   Thomas Jefferson (1743–1826)   Sally Hemings (1773–1835)

Martha   Mary   William Beverly   Harriet   James Madison   Thomas Eston

TAKEN FROM: *Frontline PBS*, "Jefferson's Blood Teacher's Guide," n.d.

able pasts. Confident in their identities, they could, like the Gibsons, cast their lot with the racial status quo.

Winch's *The Clamorgans* lacks the conceptual thrills of *The Invisible Line*. But it is a similarly impressive feat of archival reconstruction. Winch, a professor of history at the University of Massachusetts, Boston, focuses on a single mixed-race family that spent centuries litigating land claims in a case she compares to *Jarndyce v. Jarndyce* from Charles Dickens' *Bleak House*.

Her narrative is, at its heart, "a story about inheritance." The pursuit of the 18th-century real estate fortune amassed by the unscrupulous French merchant-adventurer Jacques Clamorgan entailed owning up to the other side of the family tree: Clamorgan's multiple African-American mistresses and their illegitimate offspring. Over the years, the family "straddled the shifting racial fault line" and "made and remade their identities," Winch writes—more evidence of the hazy construction of race in America.

Jacques Clamorgan was a larger-than-life scoundrel—a constantly overextended schemer whom Winch wryly describes as "too big to fail." Over the years, the courts were never really able to unravel his descendants' land claims, and Winch's readers may not make much sense of them, either. But there is wonderful social and cultural history packed between the arcana of the land disputes, including the tale of an elite St. Louis bathing establishment known as Clamorgans, where Edward, Prince of Wales, paid a pseudonymous visit in 1860.

But the most compelling story in the book—an early 20th-century melodrama fit for the stage—involves the birth of an unexpectedly dark-skinned child to a Clamorgan descendant and her equally light-skinned spouse. With other Clamorgans living and working in white enclaves in the St. Louis area passing as white, that birth had explosive consequences. One white husband, at the behest of his appalled father, sought an annulment, and two Clamorgan daughters were reassigned to black schools.

But some white neighbors remained supportive of the family—a reminder of the flexibility of communal standards. And any jury in the annulment case would have faced the daunting task of reaching a "determination of the degree of 'negro blood' . . . based on appearance." Instead, the annulment suit was abandoned, and one branch of the Clamorgan family fled their native St. Louis for Los Angeles. There, Winch reports, they changed their name to "Morgan," and "began the process of reclaiming their identity as white people."

> *"While we find a few respondents have passed as white in rare situations, the majority of respondents have, at one time or another, passed as black."*

Children of Biracial Families Today Often Choose to Pass as Black

Nikki Khanna and Cathryn Johnson

Nikki Khanna is assistant professor of sociology at the University of Vermont; Cathryn Johnson is a professor of sociology at Emory University. In the following viewpoint, the authors argue that many biracial people actively choose to pass as black to fit in with peers, avoid stigma, or gain benefits. The authors argue that the fact that so many people choose to pass as black, rather than as white, indicates that some racial stigma may be lifting from black identity, at least in some cases. They also argue that understandings of race are changing so that people of mixed race are seen, at least sometimes, as biracial rather than as black, and so may decide to "pass" or present themselves as black.

Nikki Khanna and Cathryn Johnson, "Passing as Black: Racial Identity Work Among Biracial Americans," *Social Psychology*, vol. 7, no. 4, 2010, pp. 380, 390–95. Copyright © 2010 by Sage Publications. All rights reserved. Reproduced by permission.

As you read, consider the following questions:

1. What do the authors say prevents many of the biracial people they interviewed from gaining full acceptance from whites?

2. What advantages do the authors say biracial people may gain by passing as black?

3. Why do the authors suggest that it is relatively easy for biracial people to pass as black?

Drawing on interview data with black-white biracial adults, we examine the considerable agency most have in asserting their racial identities to others. Extending research on "identity work," we explore the strategies biracial people use to conceal (i.e., pass), cover, and/or accent aspects of their racial ancestries, and the individual and structural-level factors that limit the accessibility and/or effectiveness of some strategies. We further find that how these biracial respondents identify is often contextual—most identify as biracial, but in some contexts, they pass as monoracial. Scholars argue that passing may be a relic of the past, yet we find that passing still occurs today. Most notably, we find a striking reverse pattern of passing today—while passing during the Jim Crow era involved passing as white, these respondents more often report passing as black today. Motivations for identity work are explored, with an emphasis on passing as black. . . .

Passing as Black to Fit In

Motivations for passing as white, especially during the Jim Crow era, are well documented. Less is known, however, about the motivations for passing as black. While we find a few respondents have passed as white in rare situations, the majority of respondents have, at one time or another, passed as black and they do this for several reasons—to fit in with black peers, to avoid a (white) stigmatized identity, and/or for some perceived advantage or benefit.

Not wanting to stand out, especially in adolescence, respondents often describe working to "blend in" to feel accepted by peers. In some cases, they try to fit in with both black and white peers. Kristen grew up attending a predominantly white school and a predominantly black gymnastics program, and says, "Going to school and going to the gym were just two totally different things for me. So it's like I had to switch. I was like Superman. I was kind of like Clark Kent—take off my glasses going to the gym and then put them back on when I was in school. . . . I would just kind of change. I would just do little things that I very well knew what I was doing." The "little things" included changing her clothing and speech depending upon the race of her audience (i.e., drawing on black and white cultural symbols). When asked why she altered her appearance and behavior between friends, she says, "To fit in probably. Because I wanted friends in both areas."

While some respondents employ identity strategies to "fit in" with their black *and* white peers, the majority claim that their black characteristics (e.g., dark skin) prevent their full acceptance by whites (unlike Kristen, above, who claims she looks white). Feeling thwarted by whites, many respondents pass as black to find a place with their black peers. Stephanie describes her experiences in school and says, "First grade through eighth grade I was in the same school and it was an all-black private school. So everybody there was black. . . . And all the kids . . . basically told me I was white. . . . And I got so frustrated because I wanted to fit in and they kind of made me feel like I wasn't going to fit in if I didn't go along with being totally black." As described earlier, Stephanie uses several strategies (e.g., downplaying white cultural symbols, selective association with black peers) to present a black identity. Michaela similarly managed a black identity for her black peers, and describes how she modified her speech. When asked why, she responds, "Trying to fit in with [my black peers], you try to pick up the lingo they say. I will say 'crunk this'. . . 'that's the bomb.'"

Kendra, too, passed as black in high school. Using selective disclosure, she says, "In high school, I was trying to fit in. . . . I didn't want people to know that I was half white. That I was mixed. I just wanted to be black because there was a majority of black kids there. . . . Like if [black peers] asked, I would just say I was black." Trying to fit in with black peers was a frequent theme among the majority of respondents when describing middle school and high school (and to some extent elementary school), yet this motivation appears less important beyond the high school years.

Fitting in with black peers also appeared more important for women than men in the sample; they more often describe situations in which they were discredited as black if their biracial background was revealed. [Kerry Ann] Rockquemore and [David L.] Brunsma find that biracial women often encounter negative experiences with black women because of their looks and/or biracial ancestry, and we also find that they, at times, find their blackness challenged. Describing her experiences with black women, Natasha says:

> For some [black] people, [a biracial background] is a strike against you . . . with girls, I can't escape [my white] side. It's constantly being brought up . . . they always seem to make sure to tell me I'm not really black. If I would tell someone I'm black, they would say, "No, you're mixed" . . . when people are always reminding you, "You're mixed" . . . trying to discredit you, it's hard.

Natasha is constantly reminded that she is biracial and "not really black." Olivia, too, describes how some black women do not see her as black: "I think when I was growing up, [black girls] just did not accept me as being a black girl . . . with [black] women, I still think there are some instances where they don't see me as an authentic black woman. . . ." Thus, wanting to fit in, not have their blackness discredited, nor feel contention with black peers, some respondents consciously concealed their white/biracial ancestries.

Passing as Black to Avoid a Stigmatized Identity

In the Jim Crow era, blackness was stigmatized (e.g., as inferior, backward) and is arguably stigmatized today. In describing an experience as an undergraduate, Caroline notes the stigma and says:

> I can remember when I was an undergrad, one time I got braids in my hair . . . that were down my back. And it wasn't anything dramatic and I thought it looked really nice and I liked it. And as soon as I went back to school in the city . . . I was immediately on guard when I was walking down the street. And I was like, "Oh gosh, I don't want people to think I'm black because I have these braids in my hair." . . . I was so nervous . . . that was all that went through my mind, "I don't want people to think that I'm black." . . . I know it sounds awful, but I don't want people to think that I'm stupid or that I'm bitchy or anything like that. So I didn't keep them in for very long.

Conscious about how her braids raced her as black, Caroline manipulates her phenotype (removes her braids) to avoid negative stereotypes she associates with blackness (e.g., stupidity, bitchiness).

While Caroline describes covering her black background because of stigma associated with blackness (her phenotype prevents her from passing as white), others pass as black because of stigma associated with whiteness. [Debbie] Storrs finds that multiracial women "manage their potentially discreditable nonwhite identities through identity work, including reversing the stigma associated with the nonwhiteness." In short, they stigmatized whiteness by equating it with oppression, prejudice, and discrimination, and we find that some respondents in the present study similarly stigmatize whiteness or find it stigmatized by others. Stephanie describes the negativity associated with whiteness among her black peers, and says:

[My black friends] had never been around white people before. So they only knew what their parents told them. And
they were told certain things. . . . So their parents might
have said something about a white coworker and [my
friends] would have thought all white people were bad. . . .
I'd change myself around and then I was black, so it didn't
matter anymore. . . .

Likewise, Olivia . . . covered her white ancestry in high
school to avoid stigma associated with whiteness (because her
multiracial family was known in the community, passing as
black was not an option). She downplayed her white background by tying her straight hair back as a way of distancing
herself from whites whom she perceived as "oppressive." Jackie
passes as black with her black coworkers to avoid the stigma
that she associates with whiteness. She says, "Well at work, I'm
black. That's it. No one knows that I'm half white. I don't
want to be associated with all that. [What's 'all that'?] You
know, white people think they're better. They can sometimes
be ignorant. And that's not me. You can't trust them either. I
don't want anyone to think they can't trust me." By passing as
black, she distances herself from the associated stigma of su-
periority, ignorance, and untrustworthiness.

For [Erving] Goffman, stigma is an attribute that devalues
one's identity and, most important here, it is a social con-
struct that varies situationally; it is not an objective reality,
nor a fixed characteristic of an individual. According to [Amir]
Marvasti, an ascribed status such as race or ethnicity is not inherently stigmatizing, but can become so under certain social
conditions. Clearly whiteness in most contexts is a privileged
identity and does not hold the same stigma as blackness, yet
in some contexts having white ancestry arguably carries at
least some degree of stigma. . . . In these situations, respondents perform identity work (e.g., covering their white ancestry or passing as black) to manage what they perceive as a
situationally stigmatized identity.

Passing as Black to Gain Advantages

Finally, whiteness in the slave and Jim Crow eras conferred many advantages and privileges, and three respondents describe occasionally passing as white, even today, for some perceived benefit. Beth describes a context when she passed as white via selective disclosure: "I used to be a caseworker. Some of [my white coworkers] assumed I was white and I just rolled with it . . . yeah, you're just sitting there like, 'You really don't have a clue. I'll just continue to be white, if that's what you're going to insist on.' . . . I just left it as 'I'm going to let you assume [I'm white]. And I'll go along with it.'" When asked why she allowed others to assume she is white, she describes this as a protective strategy to avoid prejudice from coworkers. Similarly, Michelle uses selective disclosure to pass as white at work, and says:

> I [identify as white] more so when it's convenient to me in corporate America. I've witnessed where white people get further than the black people. . . . And I just think in my whole experience, not just with this job but other jobs, I have to . . . put forth that I'm white. Then they're more likely to trust me. . . . I think I use it to my advantage when I need to. [In the work setting?] Yes, because I'm trying to get ahead.

While these respondents pass as white for some perceived workplace advantage, the majority (29 respondents) pass as black in other contexts for perceived advantage—in particular, on college, scholarship, financial aid, and job applications. Frequently unaware that being biracial is often sufficient for affirmative action purposes, they presented themselves exclusively as black. While Michelle describes passing as white at work to "get ahead," she also describes passing as black on college applications. Explaining why she checks the "black box," she says, "I thought maybe if I chose black, especially in college, I'd get more financial aid. I'd get more opportunities, and so I kind of thought it was to my best advantage to just say I was black." [Kerry Ann] Rockquemore and [Patricia] Arend find that a minority of their biracial respondents identify as white, but they argue that some "mixed-race individuals, who understand themselves as white, *pass for black* in order to receive social, economic, and educational opportunities" (emphasis in original). We find that the majority of respondents in this sample, who generally identify themselves to others as biracial or mixed, occasionally pass as black when they perceive some advantage in doing so.

Denise passes as black when filling out various forms and says, "[S]ometimes there are more opportunities if you're black. . . . Some are nicer to you. There are some job opportunities where you have more weight if you're a minority. And there are more scholarships." Stephanie expresses similar sentiments and says, "The funny thing is like when I applied to [college], like for affirmative action, I checked 'black.' I do not check 'other.' . . . If I'm applying for a scholarship or something, I am 'black.'" When asked how she identifies herself to others, Julie says, "I put 'other.' Or when you can check both, I put 'African American' and 'Caucasian.' But also, I would have to say that it depends on what I'm trying to do. If I'm trying to get more money from the government, I am 'African American.' There is no white aspect to me." Concealing their white backgrounds, Julie and others selectively disclose only their black backgrounds on these forms and in doing so pass as black in order to obtain education and/or employment opportunities, scholarships, and financial aid. . . .

Attitudes Toward Race Are Shifting

With generations of interracial mixing between blacks and whites and the broad definition of blackness as defined by the one-drop rule [the idea that any black ancestor makes you black], [Nikki] Khanna argues that most Americans cannot tell the difference between biracial and black. Hence, there is little difficulty when many biracial people conceal their biracial background; this is because many "blacks" also have white phenotypic characteristics (because they, too, often have white ancestry). Further, we find that biracial respondents pass as black for additional reasons—to fit in with black peers in adolescence (especially since many claim that whites reject them), to avoid a white stigmatized identity, and, in the post–civil rights era of affirmative action, to obtain advantages and opportunities sometimes available to them if they are black (e.g., educational and employment opportunities, college financial aid/scholarships).

The phenomenon of passing as black is a particularly important finding because it underscores the changing terrain of race relations and racial politics in the United States. The practice of passing as black, rather than white, suggests that blackness is arguably less stigmatized today than earlier eras of American history—at least in certain contexts. Most respondents express pride in their blackness and embrace (and often highlight through identity work) this part of their background. In fact, in some contexts, whiteness is stigmatized, which suggests a shift in how some attribute meaning to the categories of black and white.

Further, passing as black is an interesting concept in and of itself given the unique history of race in this country, and it further illuminates changes in race and politics in the United States. In previous decades, the notion of passing as black was impossible given the one-drop rule—if one had black ancestry, they did not pass as black, they *were* black. A person could only pass as white based on a concept that was inherently racist and asymmetrical (i.e., one drop of black blood made one black, but one drop of white blood did not make one white). As the one-drop rule weakens, what it means to pass is arguably undergoing modification, especially in an era where blackness (at least in some contexts) confers tangible benefits. While the notion of passing has historically conjured up images of black-white people (who were perceived as *really* black) passing as white, shifting definitions of blackness may change this and draw new attention to the concept of passing as black.

Relatedly, these findings raise questions about who is (and who is not) black. How blackness is defined is arguably undergoing revision, and this is evident within the context of affirmative action. Being biracial is often enough to qualify for these programs, which tells us that in some measure, the one-drop rule is still at work; if one checks both black and white boxes, he/she is frequently reclassified as black and is racially positioned to potentially benefit from affirmative action programs. However, because the majority of respondents are unaware of how racial data are reaggregated, they strategically conceal their white/biracial ancestries in order to present themselves as black. This may reveal a growing disjunctive regarding how blackness is defined institutionally and socially—being biracial is equated to black by admissions officers and federal agencies, yet these respondents appear to believe that being biracial is somehow different from being black (or, at the very least, that they think that *others* consider being biracial to be different from being black).

Periodical and Internet Sources Bibliography

The following articles have been selected to supplement the diverse views presented in this chapter.

Angie Chuang	"Haiti's 'Orphans' and the Transracial Adoption Dilemma," The Root, February 9, 2010. www.theroot.com.
Felicia R. Lee	"Scholars Say Chronicler of Black Life Passed for White," *New York Times*, December 26, 2010.
Thea Lim	"From a Mixed Race Child: Tips for a White Parent," *Racialicious* (blog), April 13, 2009. www.racialicious.com.
Gillian Markson	"Interracial Marriage and How It Affects Children," Families.com, June 17, 2006.
Meredith Melnick	"Passing as Black: How Biracial Americans Choose Identity," *Time*, December 16, 2010.
Ron Nixon	"Adopted from Korea and in Search of Identity," *New York Times*, November 8, 2009.
NPR	"The Parenting Dilemmas of Transracial Adoption," May 11, 2011.
Jessica Ravitz	"Transracial Adoptions: A 'Feel Good' Act or No 'Big Deal'?," CNN, May 6, 2010.
Steve Sailer	"Interesting New Book Out This Week," *Steve Sailer:iSteve* (blog), August 22, 2006. http://isteve.blogspot.com.
Thomas Chatterton Williams	"Passing for Black?," *The Root*, December 14, 2010. www.theroot.com.
Angela S. Young	"Interracial Marriage: How Does Mixed-Heritage Affect the Children," Helium, February 23, 2011. www.helium.com.

For Further Discussion

Chapter 1

1. Based on the viewpoints by Ta-Nehisi Coates, Jonathan Chait, and Christine A. Scheller, in what ways has the Republican Party reacted to a multiracial president? Do you think this has helped or hurt Republicans? What do you think the Republican Party could do to improve its standing in an increasingly multiracial America?

2. How does the viewpoint by Francesca Biller suggest that multiracial identity is changing politically in the United States? Do you think this will increase the number of multiracial individuals in politics? Explain your answer.

Chapter 2

1. Based on the viewpoints by Brooke Donald, Gail Heriot, and Richard Kahlenberg, is affirmative action an equitable policy? Explain your reasoning.

2. Laura Marcus says that immigrants should not be pushed to assimilate while Linda Chavez argues that US policies should encourage immigrants to assimilate. With which author do you agree? Explain your reasoning.

Chapter 3

1. The Pew Research Center argues that interracial marriages are becoming increasingly accepted in America. Based on the viewpoint, why do you think younger Americans are more accepting of mixed-race marriages than older generations are? Even though older Americans remain somewhat less accepting of interracial marriage than younger Americans do, do you think those over fifty will become accepting over time? Explain your reasoning.

2. Brendan O'Neill argues that interracial marriage does not change the institution of marriage. Based on the viewpoints in this chapter, do you think he would have made that same argument if he were writing fifty or sixty years ago? Explain your answer.

Chapter 4

1. Based on the viewpoints in this chapter, are biracial children disadvantaged in some situations? If so, should interracial marriages be prevented? Explain your reasoning.

2. Based on the viewpoints in this chapter, are transracial adoptees disadvantaged in some situations? If so, should transracial adoptions be prevented? Explain your reasoning.

Organizations to Contact

The editors have compiled the following list of organizations concerned with the issues debated in this book. The descriptions are derived from materials provided by the organizations. All have publications or information available for interested readers. The list was compiled on the date of publication of the present volume; the information provided here may change. Be aware that many organizations take several weeks or longer to respond to inquiries, so allow as much time as possible.

American Civil Liberties Union (ACLU)
125 Broad Street, 18th Floor, New York, NY   10004-2400
(212) 549-2500
e-mail: aclu@aclu.org
website: www.aclu.org

The American Civil Liberties Union (ACLU) is a national organization that works to defend Americans' civil rights as guaranteed by the US Constitution. It provides legal defense, research, and education. The ACLU publishes and distributes policy statements, pamphlets, and reports such as "Deportation by Default: Mental Disability, Unfair Hearings, and Indefinite Detention in the US Immigration System" and "Deane & Polyak v. Conaway—Friend-of-the-Court Brief of the NAACP Legal Defense and Education Fund on the Relevance of Interracial Marriage to Same-Sex Marriage."

American Immigration Lawyers Association (AILA)
Suite 300, 1331 G Street NW, Washington, DC   20005
(202) 507-7600 • fax: (202) 783-7853
e-mail: liaison@aila.org
website: www.aila.org

The American Immigration Lawyers Association (AILA) is the national association of more than eleven thousand attorneys and law professors who practice and teach immigration law.

Member attorneys represent those seeking residence in the United States on behalf of themselves or others. It also provides continuing legal education and professional services to its members and the public. Its website includes back issues of *Immigration Law Today*, commentary and summary of relevant court decisions and recent and pending legislation, and other resources.

Asian American Legal Defense and Education Fund
99 Hudson Street, 12th Floor, New York, NY   10013
(212) 966-5932 • fax: (212) 966-4303
e-mail: info@aaldef.org
website: http://aaldef.org

The Asian American Legal Defense and Education Fund is a national organization that protects and promotes the civil rights of Asian Americans through litigation, advocacy, education, and organizing. Its website includes annual reports, news stories, press releases, program overviews, and blogs focusing on Asian American issues.

Cato Institute
1000 Massachusetts Avenue NW
Washington, DC   20001-5403
(202) 842-0200 • fax: (202) 842-3490
e-mail: cato@cato.org
website: www.cato.org

The Cato Institute is a libertarian public policy research foundation dedicated to limiting the role of government and protecting individual liberties. It researches claims of discrimination, supports immigration, and opposes affirmative action. Cato publishes the quarterly magazine *Regulation*, the bimonthly *Cato Policy Report*, and numerous books. Its website includes numerous articles and editorials.

Center for American Progress (CAP)
1333 H Street NW, 10th Floor, Washington, DC   20005
(202) 682-1611 • fax: (202) 682-1867

e-mail: progress@americanprogress.org
website: www.americanprogress.org

Founded in 2003, the Center for American Progress (CAP) is a progressive think tank that researches, formulates, and advocates for a bold, progressive public policy agenda. CAP supports affirmative action and immigration. Its website offers information on numerous issues and provides reports such as "Affirmative Action in the United States" and "The Right of Voluntary Marriage."

Center for Immigration Studies (CIS)
1629 K Street NW, Suite 600, Washington, DC   20006
(202) 466-8185 • fax: (202) 466-8076
e-mail: center@cis.org
website: www.cis.org

The Center for Immigration Studies (CIS) is an independent, nonpartisan, nonprofit research organization. It provides immigration policy makers, the academic community, news media, and concerned citizens with information about the social, economic, environmental, security, and fiscal consequences of legal and illegal immigration into the United States. Its website includes editorials, reports, publications, court testimony, and other resources.

Families with Children from China (FCC)
website: http://fwcc.org

Families with Children from China (FCC) is a nondenominational organization of families who have adopted children from China. Its purpose is to provide a network of support for families who have adopted in China and to provide information to prospective parents, both through supporting local chapters and through Internet resources. Local chapter contact information can be found through the website. The website also includes articles on numerous aspects of the Chinese adoption process, including discussions of legislation, family stories, and current research.

Interracial Family Organization (IFO)
e-mail: team@interracialfamily.org
website: interracialfamily.org

The Interracial Family Organization (IFO) works to facilitate the cultural recognition of interracial/multicultural families and disassociate this culture from long-standing stigma by exposing and discrediting stereotypes. Its website includes blogs, essays, portraits of featured families, and other resources.

National Association of Black Social Workers (NABSW)
2305 Martin Luther King Avenue SE, Washington, DC   20020
(202) 678-4570 • fax: (202) 678-4572
e-mail: harambee@nabsw.org
website: www.nabsw.org

The National Association of Black Social Workers (NABSW), composed of people of African ancestry, is committed to enhancing the quality of life and empowering people of African ancestry through advocacy, human services delivery, and research. The organization is opposed to interracial adoption. Its website includes information about task forces, position papers, blogs, and more.

National Urban League
120 Wall Street, New York, NY   10005
(212) 558-5300 • fax: (212) 344-5332
website: www.nul.org

A community service agency, the National Urban League aims to eliminate institutional racism in the United States. It also provides services for minorities who experience discrimination in employment, housing, welfare, and other areas. Its website includes news reports and publications such as *Opportunity Journal, Urban Influence Magazine*, and others.

United States Commission on Civil Rights
1331 Pennsylvania Avenue NW, Suite 1150
Washington, DC   20425

(202) 376-7700
website: www.usccr.gov

A fact-finding body, the United States Commission on Civil Rights reports directly to Congress and the president on the effectiveness of equal opportunity programs and laws. Its website includes press releases, information on recent investigations, and numerous reports.

Bibliography of Books

Marisa A. Abrajano and R. Michael Alvarez
New Faces, New Voices: The Hispanic Electorate in America. Princeton, NJ: Princeton University Press, 2010.

Otto Santa Ana and Celeste Gonzalez de Bustamante, eds.
Arizona Firestorm: Global Immigration Realities, National Media, and Provincial Politics. Lanham, MD: Rowman & Littlefield Publishers, 2012.

Angelo N. Ancheta
Race, Rights, and the Asian American Experience. 2nd ed. New Brunswick, NJ: Rutgers University Press, 2006.

Elizabeth Anderson
The Imperative of Integration. Princeton, NJ: Princeton University Press, 2010.

Andrew Aoki and Okiyoshi Takeda
Asian American Politics. Malden, MA: Polity Press, 2008.

Eric J. Bailey
The New Face of America: How the Emerging Multiracial, Multiethnic Majority Is Changing the United States. Santa Barbara, CA: Praeger, 2013.

Jeff Biggers
State Out of the Union: Arizona and the Final Showdown over the American Dream. New York: Nation Books, 2012.

James H. Carr and Nandinee K. Kutty, eds.
Segregation: The Rising Costs for America. New York: Routledge, 2008.

Erica Chito
Childs
Fade to Black and White: Interracial Images in Popular Culture. Lanham, MD: Rowman & Littlefield, 2009.

Carl Cohen and
James P. Sterba
Affirmative Action and Racial Preference: A Debate. New York: Oxford University Press, 2003.

Jeff Gammage
China Ghosts: My Daughter's Journey to America, My Passage to Fatherhood. New York: William Morrow, 2007.

Juan Gonzalez
Harvest of Empire: A History of Latinos in America. New York: Penguin Books, 2011.

Jane Junn and
Kerry L. Haynie,
eds.
New Race Politics in America: Understanding Minority and Immigrant Politics. New York: Cambridge University Press, 2008.

Randall Kennedy
Interracial Intimacies: Sex, Marriage, Identity, and Adoption. New York: Pantheon Books, 2003.

David Paul Kuhn
The Neglected Voter: White Men and the Democratic Dilemma. New York: Palgrave Macmillan, 2007.

Kevin Noble
Maillard and Rose
Cuison Villazor
Loving v. Virginia in a Post-Racial World: Rethinking Race, Sex, and Marriage. New York: Cambridge University Press, 2012.

Donna Jackson
Nakazawa
Does Anybody Else Look Like Me?: A Parent's Guide to Raising Multiracial Children. Cambridge, MA: Perseus Books, 2003.

Carl H. Nightingale	*Segregation: A Global History of Divided Cities.* Chicago, IL: University of Chicago Press, 2012.
William Perez	*We Are Americans: Undocumented Students Pursuing the American Dream.* Sterling, VA: Stylus, 2009.
Darron Smith, Cardell K. Jacobson, Brenda G. Juárez, and Joe R. Feagin	*White Parents, Black Children: Experiencing Transracial Adoption.* Lanham, MD: Rowman & Littlefield, 2011.
Earl Smith and Angela Hattery, eds.	*Interracial Relationships in the 21st Century.* 2nd ed. Durham, NC: Carolina Academic Press, 2012.
Thomas Sowell	*Affirmative Action Around the World: An Empirical Study.* New Haven, CT: Yale University Press, 2004.
Thomas J. Sugrue	*Not Even Past: Barack Obama and the Burden of Race.* Princeton, NJ: Princeton University Press, 2010.
Peter Wallenstein	*Tell The Court I Love My Wife: Race, Marriage and Law—An American History.* New York: Palgrave Macmillan, 2004.
Adia Harvey Wingfield and Joe R. Feagin	*Yes We Can?: White Racial Framing and the Obama Presidency.* New York: Routledge, 2013.
Tim J. Wise	*Affirmative Action: Racial Preference in Black and White.* New York: Routledge, 2005.

Philip Q. Yang   *Asian Immigration to the United States.* Malden, MA: Polity Press, 2011.

Index

N